CU00842535

Ayeka

Evolving Answers to an Eternal Question

54 Torah Portions to Engage the Soul

Elisha Wolfin

Veahavta Congregation
Zichron Yaakov, Israel

Contents of Table

Introduction

"We think that when we read the Bible and discover new ideas in it, we are interpreting it, but in reality the reverse is true: the Bible that we read is actually the interpretation of the hidden Bible within our souls."

Aharon David Gordon

The Torah portions are the heartbeat of the Jewish People. Jews of every denomination and anyone who is connected to the rhythm of the weekly Torah reading knows the experience of the week being colored by the bright hues of the parasha. During any particular week, the specific parasha seems as though it is the most significant of all; the other 54 parashot fade into the background, and the current one seems to resonate miraculously with every aspect of our lives.

What is the magic of the Torah and of this weekly rhythm? How is it that words that are thousands of years old still resonate our inner experience today? How can they be as fresh and surprising every year?

In the Middle Ages the term "70 Faces of the Torah" was coined. Did Our Sages mean this literally? Does 70 simply mean "many"? Or perhaps the Rabbis actually meant "endless"?

A person, too, has at least seventy faces. One day we are more connected to one, and the next to another. One day he or she may feel one quality more strongly, and the next day another. One day our world feels like it is caving in, and the next day we may feel invincible. In this way the Torah accurately reflects and resonates the many facets of our inner world. The Torah becomes a deep, safe place in which we can process our life's journey. It enables us to observe and understand the complexities of our souls, and to grow and change.

"As water reflects the face, so the heart of man reflects the man." (Proverbs 27:19) Just as our face is reflected back to us when we look in the water, so the heart of a person standing in front of us reflects us and the state of our heart. The Torah reflects our "seventy faces". Avraham, Yoseph, Moshe, Aharon, Pharaoh, and even the Nile and Mount Sinai all reveal something hidden about ourselves, allowing a historic/mythical tale to become a dynamic and honest reflection of hidden corners of our lives.

How does this miracle happen? How does a seemingly random parasha resonate our personal inner story each week – all 7 billion of us? How does it "know"? What is the secret of the Torah's power?

The truth is I have no idea. I am entirely captivated by the Torah's magic and by its weekly heartbeat, but I do not know how it works. Not knowing is actually part of the magic, part of the miracle. We are left with a sense of great awe and amazement.

This amazement has tempted generation upon generation of Jews and non-Jews to look into this well and see themselves reflected in it. I, too, have looked, and have allowed myself to fall into its deep, life-giving waters.

Studying the Torah requires some skill. It is needed in order to be able to be fully attuned to this heartbeat. A person who is not familiar with the methodology of Torah learning will have difficulty reaching its depths, and may be disappointed at first reading. In addition to skill, an open mind and a degree of practice asking life's big questions is also required. Our Sages approached the Torah with great curiosity. Each letter stunned them. They dwelled on each minute detail, discovering in it the delights, the mysteries and the secrets of the Torah, but mostly, they discovered themselves in the process. Their curiosity led them to reveal the infinite facets of the world, of Creation, and of themselves. They did not take anything for granted. Every word raised existential thoughts. For them, the Torah that held the secrets of the universe was contained within a hard shell, and discovering those secrets required cracking that shell. Sometimes it is very hard! The modern reader who is unfamiliar with the art of the weekly Torah portion may see only the tough, daunting, seemingly-impenetrable exterior.

The goal of this book is to crack the shell that conceals the inner depth of the Torah week after week, and by doing so we are also able to remove the hard shell that surrounds our lives, and reach our inner core.

As a child I very much disliked Bible classes. I found them entirely shell-like, dry, and inanimate. And then, one day, in the spring of 1981, two weeks before our final graduation exam, a substitute teacher arrived in class, replacing our regular teacher who had gone on maternity leave. Those were days of intense preparation, but instead of having us memorize a phenomenal amount of material; this new teacher – a secular kibbutznik like myself at the time – cracked the dull shell of the Torah for me for the first time in my life. She introduced us to Avraham of "Lech Lecha" in a way that I had never known. On that day Avraham went from being a cold and irritating literary figure to "Avraham Avinu", Avraham, my father, the lively and enlivening guide of life. I was 17 years old – the same age Yoseph was when he set out on his journey. For the first time in my life I discovered dormant layers of life within me reflected in the verses of the Torah.

The final exams were over and life took me in other directions. For many years I did not come back to the Torah, but that one-time meeting with its potential depths left a strong, sweet imprint on my memory.

In my thirties, far from Israel, while living on a houseboat in the San Francisco Bay, I met the spiritual teachers who brought me back to the Torah. More precisely, they didn't bring me back to the Torah, but to myself. The Torah provided the signposts on my journey home. While the Torah was one, each teacher revealed different and unique facets, introducing me to some of the 70 faces concealed in the Torah.

This book is my humble attempt to discover some of the many layers within the Torah and within myself. Through it, I am practicing our Sages' classic art of questioning, wondering, investigating, and finding answers in the Torah.

I accept our Sages' basic precept that the Torah is truth, that there is nothing random or coincidental in it, and that it is the blueprint of the universe. Just as there are no real mistakes in life, there are no mistakes in the Torah. If a difficulty arises from the text, be it technical, linguistic, or any other, we might be tempted to dismiss it as a mistake in the script, a case of banality or a description of a primitive custom of long ago. But in doing so we would be missing what the Torah has to offer us. Instead, let us agree for the moment to suspend disbelief, to engage, and to demand deeper and more significant answers from the text. In this way we are guaranteed to discover new depths, new answers, and fresh, life-giving water.

Acknowledgements

There are many people I would like to thank.

First of all, I would like to thank Shlomo and Sharona Maital. Professor Shlomo Maital encouraged me to collect my weekly writing on the Torah portion into a book. He prodded gently and made the printing of this book possible.

I am grateful to the Rosenberg family, who, for the past four years, has made the translation into English possible. Every Drasha that goes out to my Hebrew-speaking readers is also translated into English. What you will be reading in this book is edited versions of my weekly English drashot.

I would like to thank Amotz Sorek for editing; my mother, Tamar Wolfin, for proofreading; Tami Kruger, for comments and insights; Aviva Freedberg for detailed technical work; Sigal Garibi, who, together with my mother and Tami, chose the drashot included in this collection (because there are many more).

I would like to thank my faithful readers who respond to my writing each week, even though it is emailed just moments before Shabbat.

I would like to thank my dear community, Veahavta, and its chairwomen, Paula Friedland and Dafna Kalmar. We established the Kehillah, eight adventurous families, 14 years ago, and have continued to grow and develop ever since.

I would like to thank everyone who attends my bi-weekly class on the Torah portion. They come eager to confront the text, determined to glean another spark of truth, another drop of living water, another hidden layer.

I wish to lovingly acknowledge the memory of my grandmother, Linny Bielski, z"l, who argued with me, insisting for years that the answers are in the Torah, and that one day I would discover them.

I wish to thank my wife, Ronit Shefi-Wolfin, who has always been and remains *the* spiritual teacher, and my partner on my journey. Thank you, Ronit, for thirty years of love and marriage.

Finally, I thank the Creator, whom I hear on a daily basis asking us "Ayeka?", "Where are you?", and when He sees that we do not know how to answer, usually blaming the woman or the serpent, He graciously provides us with the keys to ancient doors, a map to hidden treasures, and tools with which to dig wells and find springs of life-giving water, so that we are able to answer repeatedly, "Hineni!", "Here I am!"

Zichron Yaakov, 2018

Translator's Note

I have used three sources for the English quotes of the biblical texts:

The online translation of Machon Mamre (the Mamre Institute); the Etz Hayim Torah and Commentary of the USCJ, produced by the JPS; and my own suggestions based on my understanding of Elisha's reading of the text.

Each chapter of this book contains one **drasha** on the weekly Torah portion. The root of the word drasha is "to demand", as in "demanding from the ancient text a plausible interpretation." The term for **Torah portion** is **parasha.** Parasha means both "episode" and "explanation".

I have used masculine form in relation to God for the sake of brevity and uniformity. God has many names – they are mentioned throughout this book in various contexts. Where significant, the precise Hebrew name of "God" or "the Lord" has been transliterated to reflect the particular name used.

Where possible, the writing is gender-neutral. This is complicated by the fact that Hebrew is not. Every effort has been made to make the text as inclusive as possible.

It is our hope that this book will inspire English readers. Because it was originally written in Hebrew for a primarily-Israeli audience, it alludes at times to Israeli current events. Understanding these events is not essential to understanding the message of the drashot, but we wanted to include them because they are part of the Jewish Israeli culture and spice that characterizes our congregation.

Regarding spelling and transliteration: All names have been transliterated so that they appear as they are pronounced in Hebrew (Genesis is Bereishit, Eve is Chava, Rebecca is Rivka and so on). The letter "chet" (ח) has been transliterated as "ch" in order to distinguish it from "h" (ה). The names of the books of the Bible (Tanach) appear in their English form.

The premise of Torah study is that the rich linguistic forms of the original Hebrew text offer the opportunity for many interpretations. Each word, phrase, sentence, and sequence may be understood in myriad ways - the more the better (and the richer). These interpretations, as well as being a linguistic art, became the basis of Rabbinic Judaism and of Jewish culture and thought. It is therefore a very heavy responsibility to choose the English version of any of these holy words. I am both honored and humbled by the opportunity to take part in this ancient endeavor of biblical interpretation.

Tami Lombard Kruger

Bereishit – The Mark of Cain

Here we are, "Achrei Hachagim" (after the holidays), a momentous time in Israel. If all has gone well, we should be able and willing to take a fresh look at the ancient words of the Torah, finding new meaning and new inspiration in them as we begin a new yearly cycle.

I would like to revisit the original, prototypical "failure" - the first son of mankind, Cain.

Cain, having murdered his brother Hevel in an apparent fit of jealousy, is banished from the earth and cursed until the seventh generation, although he receives a shield of divine protection. Cain's genealogy ends at the seventh generation, at which point the Torah details the lineage of the offspring of Adam and Chava's third son, Shet.

On the other hand, Cain is also described as the father of all human inventions. He and his offspring build the first city (perhaps because they were forbidden from dwelling on the land). The Bedouin culture of nomads and shepherds are also Cain's offspring (again, perhaps because they could not be farmers). Another descendant invented music and musical instruments. Was this also in response to the same punishment? Yet another developed tools and weapons made of iron:

"And Cain knew his wife; and she conceived, and bore Chanoch; and he built a city, and called the name of the city after the name of his son Chanoch. And unto Chanoch was born Irad; and Irad begot Mehuyael; and Mehuyael begot Methushael; and Methushael begot Lamech. And Lamech took two wives; the name of one was Adah,

and the name of the other Tzillah. And Adah bore Yaval; he was the father those who dwell in tents and have cattle. And his brother's name was Yuval; he was the father of all who handle the harp and pipe. And Tzillah, she also bore Tuval-cain, the forger of every cutting instrument of brass and iron; and the sister of Tuval-Cain was Na'amah." (Bereishit 4:17-22)

We are used to considering Cain the epitome of evil who deserves the curse he receives, yet what we read here doesn't sound like a curse, but more like a great blessing! What happened?

Professor Nechama Leibowitz, the late sister of Yisha'ayahu Leibowitz and an esteemed Torah scholar in her own right, bequeathed to us a unique methodology for approaching each parasha. She brings a unique interpretation of the story of Cain, quoting a very unusual source, Benno Yaakov. Yaakov is not often quoted, perhaps because he is identified with the Reform Movement. Although Nechama (as she was known) was a very observant Jew, she sought wise interpretations wherever they were to be found. She wrote: "In his (*Yaakov's*) interpretation of Bereishit… the story of Cain completes the original sin of Adam. Therefore, Cain's punishment parallels Adam's punishment. The interpreter Benno Yaakov ends his explanation there thus: 'Cain's sin – its relation to Adam's sin is like the relation between the first and second set of Tablets.'"

In what way are the two great sins of this parasha – eating from the Tree of Knowledge and the first murder – parallel? And what is the similarity between them and the first and second Tablets? As was her way, Nechama Leibowitz leaves these questions unanswered and challenges us to find the answers ourselves, which we will try to do here.

The Torah, in its brilliance, conveys two levels of existence or consciousness:

The first is that of Hevel, in which gifts are always accepted, but contains no life. It is the world of angels – of perfect people who have never sinned because they have never created anything. This is a world like the Garden of Eden, in which there is no shame, no urges. Everyone is naked, but because there is nothing titillating about this and there is no urge to procreate. King Shlomo uses the same word – the name Hevel – to describe a world in which all is in vain, for naught - in Kohelet, which we just read over the Succot holiday.

The second level is that of Cain, in which there is struggle, jealousy, anger, complaint, and violence. But it is also the world of miraculous human creation and invention. We find Cain's world difficult to accept, because we know that it is wrong to be jealous, to complain or to hit… But within this wrong, human creativity is to be found. In order to invent and create, it seems curiosity is not enough. One also has to be a little bit disgruntled – enough so as to make an effort to change the situation.

Parallel to these two levels of existence we can find in the parasha two beginnings: the first is THE story of Creation, described in chapters one and two of Genesis, and the second evolves from Adam and Chava's sin.

The first Creation was of a perfect world in which all was good, even very good; perhaps too good; so good that there was no need to evolve or change. This is like the world of Hevel. In the second story, the world was created full of difficulty and a sense of deficiency; a world that necessitated the sweat of one's brow to raise food, and pain and hardship in giving birth. The deficiencies of this world enabled human brilliance and creativity to flourish, yet it is the world of Cain. How can this be? Has the villain become the hero?

The first sin, following the first version of Creation, is punished by banishment from the world of perfection to the reality of working the earth, hunting and shepherding. The second sin - Cain's - follows the second version of Creation, and there Cain is punished by banishment from any connection to the earth, into the realm of human creativity.

How are the Tablets connected in this parable? The first Tablets are the words of the Living God, written by the hand of God on Divine tablets. When Moshe comes down and sees the Golden Calf, those tablets become "hevel havalim", like a puff of air that has no substance. The second set of Tablets are human, written by Moshe, dealing with human frailty, beliefs, urges, relationships, the need for rest (Shabbat) and the human inclination to be violent, to lie, and to steal. That second set of Tablets becomes ours, and it is those Tablets that have survived throughout history.

This completes the comparison between the two types of beginning, the two sins and the two sets of Tablets. An important point has not yet been resolved, though: Why is Cain's lineage not mentioned beyond the seventh generation? Did it dsappear?

The Ramban provides an interesting explanation: He suggests that there was no decree of annihilation at the end of seven generations, and that Cain's offspring simply became all of humanity, making all of us his descendants! Don't Cain's faults sound familiar? We, too, are filled with jealousy, hatred, complaints, criticism and fear. Like Cain, we wander in discontent – building, destroying, creating and inventing.

16

When the serpent tells Chava that she and Adam would not die if they ate from the Tree of Knowledge he is right, in the human, second, Cain sense. Indeed, they eat and they don't die. But in the Hevel, Eden, first sense, the snake does lie – the perfection of Eden becomes unattainable, and the awareness of mortality is created.

Following this line of thought, God's reference to the punishment of Cain for seven generations is correct in the second sense and Cain's descendants are not mentioned. However, in the deeper, first sense, God or the Torah actually instilled "Cain-ness" in all of humanity. We wander the earth with the mark of Cain upon our brow, sometimes hidden, sometimes obvious, always a source of vulnerability and shame.

Hevel, the righteous one, may he rest in peace.

Cain, may he live a long, creative life.

And Seth, the third brother? Is he able to find a synthesis between these two modes of being - the mode of Hevel's Oneness, and the mode of Cain's duality? The next 53 parashot of the Torah point towards a possible answer. It is this synthesis that we are after, in the deepest, existential sense, seeking to fully live our lives in the dualistic world, and anchor our consciousness in the Oneness from which all emerged.

Thank you for joining us for another cycle of Torah portions!

Parashat Noah: The Wisdom of Not Knowing

It has been a very trying couple of weeks. It is hard enough coping with the fear and terror all around us; it is so much more painful to read and listen to the narrative portrayed outside of Israel.

This drasha is not about current events. It was written many days before the latest cycle of violence broke out, but it echoes the deep questions many of us are asking these days.

The more the Middle Eastern reality surprises us with newer forms of evil, the more we question our fundamental truths. When the U.S. State Department blames Israel for using excessive force while protecting civilians from innocent-looking assassins; when the world buys chairman Abbas' blood libel of an Israeli execution of a 13 year old Palestinian boy, while the terrorist who severely wounded a 13 year old Israeli boy is alive and recuperating at Hadassah Hospital, getting the best treatment available in the Middle East... It feels as if something is terribly wrong.

Could it be that our entire value system is flawed?

What is it with God's world?

Is He around?

Is He listening?

I will now switch to the drasha about Parashat Noah, which, as I said earlier, was written many days before the current events broke out. However, since the Parasha raises similar questions, I hope that it can help ease some of the pain that we are feeling.

Let us begin. Parashat Noah.

Is the God we believe in wrong sometimes?

Does the God we believe in learn from experience the way we humans do?

Does the God we believe in act with clear and definite measures of justice? If so, how can it be that the innocent are hurt (in the Flood, for example)?

Are we allowed to complain to the God we believe in about the way He or She rules the world, if at all?

Is the God we believe in all-powerful, or is His power limited? If so, by what?

Is the God we believe in involved with what happens here and now? If so, why doesn't He prevent terrible things from happening?

These are very common and well-known questions. It is impossible to read our parasha this week without asking some of these tough questions.

Before the flood:

"And the LORD saw that the wickedness of man was great in the earth, and that every imagination of the thoughts of his heart was only evil continually. And it repented the LORD that He had made man on the earth, and it grieved Him at His heart. And the LORD said: 'I will blot out man whom I have created from the face of the earth; both man, and beast, and creeping thing, and fowl of the air; for it repents Me that I have made them." (Genesis 6:5-7)

After the flood:

"...and the LORD said in His heart: 'I will not again curse the earth any more for man's sake; for the inclination of man's heart is evil

19

from his youth; neither will I again smite any more everything living, as I have done." (Bereishit 8:21)

Does the God of this parasha regret having created the world?

Was it a divine mistake?

Does God regret having destroyed the world with the Flood?

Was that another divine mistake?

And...

Why are innocent animals also destroyed?

Why does God allow Cain to murder Hevel? Why does He allow humans to sin? Why does He enable the world to deteriorate to the point of no return?

What kind of theology lies at the core of this week's parasha?

Theology is a personal thing. Deep within each person's unconscious there is some form of theology which guides his or her decisions, even if it has never been formulated. Having a theology suggests that we know a thing or two, that we carry deep-seated truths.

Do we?

One point of view is that there are indeed definite answers. Another opinion is that we really don't know anything at all. According to this point of view, all of the questions above are irrelevant, because we have absolutely no way of knowing anything at all – not about God, nor about His sense of justice or injustice, or even the fact of His existence.

Personally, I am a big believer in the second version – that in which we know absolutely nothing. Often - very often in fact - I sense a glimmer of The Divine Truth (caps intended), only to discover that it was only the outer shell of a deeper truth, and that deeper truth was much different from its superficial manifestation.

What can be learned, then, from Parashat Noah?

Our Sages state many times that "the Torah speaks in human language", meaning that even though it is the word of the Living God, it is expressed in a way that humans can understand, both linguistically and ideologically. This is a very significant statement, because it means that the version we read is like an "abridged version" for limited human consumption, and forestalls attempts to understand the "unabridged version" with our human minds. The language in which the Torah is written is almost like a code, made to be understood at the human level, but containing Divine truths that are beyond human understanding.

Our limitation is necessary for our very existence: if we could blend into the Divine (and many of us would be inclined to seize the opportunity), we would cease to exist! Our limited brains, then, are a filter, an adapter, a transformer that keeps us from blowing a fuse of Divine light. As human Googles, we search our brain frantically for answers to our burning questions of faith, in order to make sense and order where we would otherwise perceive none.

Those of us who love the Torah and are addicted to studying it, do so because we can sense that beneath the reams of human words a deeper truth remains hidden, and a deeper one beneath that one as well. We dig, search and re-search. Along the way, we may find gold and precious stones, but we hear that soft and persistent voice that calls to us from deep within the Torah, telling us to keep going, to look deeper and more thoroughly, and we do, because the entire point is the learning, the digging, not reaching a destination. Anything attained is no more than a deceptive and partial truth.

This is why we cannot conclude anything about God's identity, and a degree of humility is required of us: we must accept that we know nothing, and continue to engage in the process of learning. Only then can we be open to new discoveries which will hold momentary truths which will be clear, and then escape us once again.

Shabbat Shalom, a Shabbat of not knowing, and being open to new discoveries; and mostly, a Shabbat in which we don't give up digging in the depths in search of precious stones, of peace, of human coexistence.

Parashat Lech Lecha: The World of Avraham

Welcome to Avraham's world!

In one of the toughest, most touching moments in this parasha, Avraham expresses his pain to God. It is all the more poignant because it is such a rare occurrence.

"After these things [after Lot, Avraham's nephew, and possible heir, leaves to settle in S'dom] *the word of the LORD came to Abram in a vision, saying: 'Fear not, Abram, I am your shield, your reward shall be exceedingly great.' And Abram said: 'O Lord GOD, what will You give me, seeing I go hence childless. Perhaps he, who shall inherit me, and be the possessor of my house, is Eliezer of Damascus?' And Abram said* [furthermore]: *'Behold, to me You have given no seed, and no one born in my house is to be my heir.'* "(Bereishit 15:1-3)

It seems at first as though Avraham is complaining: "You know God, I've done all You've asked me to do, and you keep making me promises of continuity… Thanks! But with all due respect, I'm already in my eighties, Lot has just abandoned me, and the only heir I have so far is my servant. So what in the world are you talking about?"

Is Avraham asking for a child? Until now Avraham and Sarah have never have made such a request, nor have they ever complained that they have none. Yitzchak and Rivka, Yaakov and Rachel - in stark contrast to Avraham and Sarah - not only ask, they demand heirs. Rachel and Rivka, who were unique in being beloved, demand of their husbands to use their influence with the Creator of children that He make them fruitful. Yitzchak indeed asks on behalf of his wife.

Yaakov doesn't. He reacts to his wife's pressure with an outburst: "What do you want from me? Do I look like God to you?" Therefore it is striking that for the first time, Avraham expresses his dismay.

Why now?

What is missing in order to fully understand this passage is Avraham's tone of voice when he says: "Behold, you have not blessed me with heirs." Imagining the tone of voice is a Midrash unto itself, a profound interpretation. Here are two options:

"Okay, so what can you possibly give me? Another challenge? Another hurdle? Another test? Another fright? You are always promising blessings, and meanwhile all you have sent my way are difficulties. Can you please fulfill your promise? Time is running out, you know!"

Or maybe: "You know what? I don't want any blessings – no promises, nothing! I agreed to this insane journey You sent me on because You promised me continuity (progeny). For years I have followed you blindly, dragging my poor wife with me, living the life of a nomad, all because of the promise of a child. Dear God, are you at all sure you're planning on fulfilling Your promise? Is that still the plan?"

I don't think either scenario is correct. Avraham would not use that tone of voice, not even in moments of crisis. It is just not in his character. As I read the passage over and over I begin to hear another voice, one that sounds more authentically like Avraham and consistent with his personality thus far:

"Thank you! I truly thank you for all of the blessings and promises. They are very consoling. But, there is one piece of the puzzle missing. You keep telling me about all of these grand plans that will occur through my progeny, but our biological clocks have stopped ticking many years ago. My wife and I are old and our only heir is my servant. I'm not complaining, nor have I ever. I'm not worried about myself - I'm fine. So is Sarah. We don't need a thing. We did not embark on this journey in order to be rewarded. I heard Your voice and I followed. But I am concerned about You! You tell me about great plans, but so far I have no child who can implement them. I have a servant. He's really wonderful and he's loyal. What a blessing! Did you mean him? If not, please explain your plan."

Yes, I am sure this was the tone of Avraham's voice. I can't imagine another.

This kind of selfless, blind sense of mission is almost unimaginable in our modern world; perhaps even dangerous. We know how much blind faith can be a frightening force. But I also know many cultural heroes who made their contribution with the same kind of selflessness, sometimes related to religious fervor and sometimes not. Three modern examples that come to mind are Henrietta Szold, Chayim Nachman Bialik, and Menachem Mendel Schneerson, the last Lubavitcher Rebbe.

I would like to suggest that deep within most of us – or perhaps all of us – we are driven by higher motives than those that are apparent. When we look at our life journey we see things we did for money, for power, for honor, or just to prove we can. But if we delve deeper, we will discover that beneath all of these superficial desires there is an authentic sense of mission. Raising children is certainly one of them.

Our era, which is known for its "I-me-mine" centeredness, is actually not as it seems. I truly believe that every human being, in his or her heart of hearts, wants to fulfill a mission that we were brought into the world to accomplish. I truly believe that this drive, which we tend to call "self-actualization", is actually just a brilliant cover for a plan far grander.

This is why the parasha is called "Lech Lecha". Many have discussed the repetition of the word לך in the name of the Parasha. In Hebrew, Lech and Lecha are spelled the same way, and without vowels they are identical, suggesting that one may be redundant. Our Sages and later Hassidic rabbis explained that the second Lech(a) means "go towards yourself", in the sense of "be yourself, completely! You are complete, you are enough, so don't try and escape or hide behind one ideology or another. You are it!" The great prophets of our tradition were called to be themselves, to fulfill their own destiny, to use their own words and their unique skills, with God's help.

Yonah, the prophet who tried to resist, found that he couldn't. None of us can. When we attempt to escape ourselves, we encounter great misery. We wander around thinking we are not good enough, not _____ enough (we can all fill in the blank with the words we use most often to put ourselves down) and we are tormented. Not fulfilling our mission is considered a great sin! (The word for sin – חטא – also means missing the mark or missing one's mission...)

Returning to Avraham's dismay - God once again promises him that it is from his loins that descendants will come. The next verse is *"And because he put his trust in the LORD, He reckoned it to his merit."* (Bereishit 15: 6) It is not clear who the second he/He is: God thought well of Avraham, or Avraham continued to think well of God. Either way, this is the first time that the concept of belief appears.

Rabbi Shimshon Rafael Hirsch, explains Avraham's belief in an extraordinary way: Avraham did not believe someone or something. He believed IN something. He goes on to remind us that the root of

26

the words "belief" and "art" is the same (אמן). The artist is one who creates, and Avraham believes in The Creator completely. Avraham believes that God's creation is complete, and therefore his barrenness or fertility is part of the Creator's plan, and he is not concerned.

This, then, is the world of Avraham, the father of our nation. From him we learn that when we are genuinely "I-me-mine" centered, when we are willing to trust our God-given traits, we are really God-centered, knowingly or unknowingly. The difference between Avraham and the rest of us is that he was truly Self-centered, while we are more often than not Ego-centered. It is our task, then, to be true to ourselves, to be loyal to ourselves. Through our I-centeredness, God fulfills His plan. When we are AUTHENTICALLY "Self-centered", we are less "ego-centered". The difference is huge, and takes a lot of work, training, Self-acceptance, and faith.

Parashat Vayera:
Examine Your Vision, and God May Appear

This Shabbat we come to the most painful and moving story in the entire Torah – the description of the birth and sacrifice of Yitzchak.

"Painful" and "moving" are very real emotions; nevertheless, they are entirely a matter of perception. Most would agree that this story is difficult to digest. My approach is that if a story is difficult, it calls on us to re-examine it, to look deeper. So let's look again, re-examine, and see it with fresh eye. Perhaps the pain will prove easier to bear. Perhaps even… joyful!

The parasha is called Vayera, which means "and (God was) seen/revealed. And indeed, seeing and observing are the central theme of this parasha. Here are a few examples:

1. At the beginning of the parasha Avraham is sitting at the entrance of his tent in the heat of the day, and God is revealed to him. The parasha then goes on to tell us of the arrival of three people, whom we later understand to be Divine messengers.
   In what way is God revealed? What does Avraham see? It is unclear from the text whether Avraham sees God or sees messengers. Avraham even addresses the three messengers in the single tense. Does he realize they are angels? What do angels look like? What does he see?

   *"And the LORD **appeared** to him by the Terebinths of Mamre, as he sat in the tent door in the heat of the day; and he **lifted up his eyes** and **looked**, and, lo, three men stood over against him* [are they God appearing in human form, or do they appear only after God has appeared to Avraham and therefore unrelated to God's

28

appearance?]*; and when he **saw** them, he ran to meet them from the tent door, and bowed down to the earth, and said: 'My lord* [which can translate as either "my Lord" – i.e. God - or "my lord" – i.e., esteemed man, or "my lords" – i.e., distinguished people]*, if now I have found favor in **your sight*** [your in the singular]*, pass not away, I pray you, from your servant'"* [pass, you, and your, are all in the singular form in the Hebrew text]. (Bereishit 18:1-3)

The Torah has no vowels or punctuation, so if one changes the commas and the vowels, the entire interpretation changes. Who, then, is Avraham addressing? What does he see?

2. Cut to S'dom: The angels who come to remove Lot and his family from the city prior to its destruction are met by a nasty mob who gather outside Lot's house and demand that he hands over the men who have come to visit:
"And they called to Lot, and said to him: 'Where are the men that came in to you this night? Bring them out to us, that we may know them.'… And they drew near to break the door... And they [the angels] *smote the men that were at the door of the house with **blindness**, both small and great; so that they wearied themselves to **see** the door*." (Genesis 19:8-11)

3. Still in S'dom, before fleeing, the angels warn Lot and his family, *"Escape for your life; **look** not behind you… But his wife **looked** back from behind him, and she became a pillar of salt." (19:17,26)*

Why not look back? Are there things that we shouldn't see lest we become insane? What did Lot's wife see? Was it a flash of light, or some horror? Or perhaps it is simply not a good idea to look back and get swept away by nostalgia?

4. Back in the tent, Yitzchak is born, and it is Sarah's turn to see something disturbing:

    *"And Sarah **saw** the son of Hagar the Egyptian, whom she had borne to Avraham, Metsachek [unclear what this word is, perhaps making fun of… or even engaging promiscuously]. Wherefore she said to Avraham: 'Cast out this bondwoman and her son ... And the thing was very grievous in Avraham's **sight** on account of his son. And God said to Avraham: 'Let it not be grievous in your **sight** ..."* (Genesis 21:9-12)

    It is not clear what it is that Sarah sees, but whatever it is, Avraham doesn't see it, and God does.

5. And then it is Hagar's turn to see and not to see:

    *"And Avraham arose up early in the morning, and took bread and a bottle of water, and gave it to Hagar, putting it on her shoulder, and the child, and sent her away... And she went, and sat herself down far away from him [Yishmael], as it were a bow-shot; for she said: **'Let me not look** upon the death of the child.'... And God **opened her eyes**, and she **saw** a well of water…"*

    (Bereishit 1:14-19)

    Was the well there previously and Hagar did not see it? Do we get to see only that which we are able to see at any given time?

6. The final, most challenging example is the sacrifice of Yitzchak:

    *"On the third day Avraham **lifted up his eyes**, and **saw** the place afar off... And Yitzchak spoke to Avraham his father, and said: 'My father.' And he said: 'Here am I, my son.' And he said: **'Behold** the fire and the wood; but where is the lamb for a burnt-offering?' And Avraham said: 'God **will show** Himself the lamb*

*for a burnt-offering, my son... And Avraham **lifted up his eyes, and looked**, and behold behind him a ram caught in the thicket by his horns. And Avraham went and took the ram, and offered him up for a burnt-offering in the stead of his son. And Avraham called the name of that place Adonai-**yir'eh**; as it is said to this day: 'In the mount where the LORD **is seen**.' "*(Bereishit 22:4-14)

What do all of these examples tell us about sight?

First and foremost, that our entire experience of life is determined by our vision, and our vision is entirely subjective, it is completely biased. Objective sight does not exist, and what one sees has little to do with reality.

Second, that if we can't see a way out of a situation it may just be that we are simply not "really" looking. There is always a way out, but our conditioning may be blinding us. There is never a "right way" to look at things, only many possible points of view, and it is our choice to find the vision that frees us, that redeems us from painful situations.

Third, Parashat Vayera teaches us that if there is such a thing as "objective" vision, it is that in which God is seen beyond the external façade …

Rabbi Shimshon Rafael Hirsch explains the sentence "And the Lord appeared to him..." as: no place/thing is ever devoid of God's presence, but not every person SEES it. God is everywhere, all of the time, God, if you like, is the "objective reality", but we are not always able to see God or the path that we must take.

This is a profound statement! It leaves us with the responsibility to work on our vision! Hence, when we see something disturbing and are unable to change it, at least not right away (and there are many examples in current events), perhaps we are asked to re-examine our vision:

Can we see God in the picture? If not, then we are not yet seeing clearly at all!

Parashat Chayei Sarah:
The Father, the Mother, and the Spirit of the Slave

The two most challenging things we are required to do in our lives have nothing to do with our careers. Our career is what we do when not attending the truly serious topics in life: parenting and personal relationships.

I don't know if this is the way it has to be, but this is the way it is.

Our parasha begins with the death and burial of Sarah, the mother of our nation, and ends with the death and burial of Avraham, the father of our nation. Most of the parasha, though, deals with the story of finding a wife for their son, Yitzchak.

I am going to make a very generalizing statement, but I mean it to be archetypical rather than stereotypical. The roles of father and mother do not necessarily describe the actual division within a family, but rather the role each one fills.

Avraham and Sarah completely fulfill their roles in the world, and they depart in the fullness of time. Sarah's role is to bring her son into the world, to raise him, and to provide him with the optimal conditions in which to fulfill his role. But it is Avraham who gives his son his purpose. He teaches him to know God and gives him God's blessing; and God's blessing is the purpose of humankind in this world!

Every child and every individual has a unique blessing, even if we resist receiving it. This is because in order to receive a blessing we must "earn" it, and this is not easy. It is usually a difficult and painful process.

The process begins with a challenging, prolonged stage of guidance by our parents, ending with a kind of wrenching process of letting our children and our parents go, and pursuing our own blessings. The biblical story relates these clearly:

> We know nothing about Avraham's mother. She probably fulfilled her role well, because Avraham is well-prepared for his life's journey. But it is his father who gives him his purpose. Contrary to the popular midrashim about Terach, Avraham's father, it is he, and not Avraham, who leaves his country and his father's house and begins on a journey of Lech Lecha at the end of Parashat Noah.

> We are well-acquainted with Yitzchak's parents: His mother, after bringing him into the world, gives him his name, nurses him, and paves his way by banishing his brother and rival. She then passes him on to Avraham for the continuation of his upbringing.

> Avraham's task begins with listening to Sarah both in giving Yitzchak his name and in sending Yishmael away. Avraham's biggest role is in the Akeida. He gets ready to sacrifice his son on an altar to God, thereby preparing him to continue in his father's path of deepening the (actual and metaphoric) wells which Avraham has dug with great effort. Every parent prepares to sacrifice his or her child to one destiny or another!

The other stage in the process of earning one's blessings is that of creating adult relationships, and the story of finding a wife for Yitzchak is a central theme in this parasha.

> Establishing couplehood takes a lot of work. There are few creatures in nature that live as couples, and in most cases

these function out of instinct rather than conscious decision. Finding and establishing couplehood involves so many mutual expectations - both conscious and unconscious – each one capable of destroying a relationship. There is one's ego, without which nothing is possible, but too much of which can cause misery. There are many and sometimes conflicting desires. There are world views instilled by our parents, which differ based on culture. And there are the expectations of each one's role in a relationship.

Reproduction is understandable – it is part of nature – but the human expectation of creating a different kind of bond is very surprising! It is not surprising, therefore, that the first time it is mentioned in the Torah it is as "helpmates". In Hebrew the term is "ezer kenegdo", literally meaning "an aide against him." It is as if to say that the aid or aide may take the form of an opposing force.

There is a wonderful story told in Bereshit Rabba (Midrashim on Bereshit) about a woman who wondered what God did after creating the world. Rabbi Yehuda Bar Simon told her that He has been busy making matches ever since. The woman thought that this was a very easy job, and was surprised by the notion that it would involve Divine powers. She then tried her hand at it and experienced great failure. Following this, she admitted that it wasn't as easy as she thought, agreeing with Rabbi Yehuda Bar Simon's description that making good matches was as difficult as parting the Red Sea. Therefore, it requires Divine power and intervention.

The parting of the Red Sea is a wonderful but confusing metaphor. Parting rather than bringing together? An ever-shifting sea rather than stability? We always hope for peace and comfort within our personal relationships. We dream of happily-ever-after for everyone. God, on the other hand, is not familiar with this concept. God's method is "ezer keneged", meaning that an element of opposition will always be necessary for continued development. Still waters may run deep, but they can also get very stagnant and murky.

But the Divine plan causes continuous ripples and friction, because only through these is there life, growth, and continuity. Therefore, personal relationships require continuous work, even if they were "Made in Heaven".

One explanation for the difficulty inherent in relationships is that each individual is a world unto him or herself, and finding a match requires understanding of endless details that are beyond human and even artificial intelligence. What seems compatible on the surface may end up feeling dull, or the "ezer kenegdo" might be too opposing. Likewise, opposites who seem incompatible may turn out to be extremely compatible on a level beyond our human comprehension.

The second explanation, which is less obvious, appears in the story of Creation. The process of creation can be read as God's Oneness breaking up into infinite pieces, turning the One into the many, or - as spiritual teachers often refer to it - into dualism. Matchmaking, then, is the art of reinstating Oneness from the duality. As it says in Tehillim 68:7 - *"God makes the solitary to dwell in a house; "* meaning He brings back what is separate or solitary into a house, a unity. This task of reinstating unity among entire worlds by making matches may only be done by the Power which created them to begin with.

Eliezer is sent on this mission for Yitzchak, because as a loyal, archetypical servant, he can maintain the distance required for such a task and allow Divine wisdom to do the job. He does not trust his "taste" or his personal opinions. As Avraham's servant, he knows what the general criteria are for making the choice: diligence, generosity, hospitality, and respect for all people. Beyond these, Eliezer leaves the matchmaking to God, and God responds. (It is this context that the word "love" appears for the first time in the Torah, implying that when the matchmaking is completed precisely, it creates a form of love perhaps less familiar to us today.)

This parasha reminds us that while matches may be made in heaven, they still involve a lot of hard work. But it is the most important work we can do. Our parenting, too, will result in division, enabling our children to make their own way and to bring their own blessings to the world.

At the end of the day, the business of parenting, finding mates and establishing other close relationships contains great mystery. The rhymes and reasons are hidden from our very limited understanding, but we are assured that we each have a role, a purpose, and a blessing.

Parashat Toldot: In Pursuit of a Blessing

Parashat Toldot is my birthday parasha, and it is one of my favorites. In it the first twins, Eisav and Yaakov (Eisav and Yaakov), are born. I like them both, even yough Eisav will forever remain for me the ultimate example of "the other". Also, Yaakov will later be called Israel, and this is my middle name.

The word Toldot appears for the first time at the end of the story of Creation. It is used to sum up an amazing feat – the creation of Man.

"This is the book of the generations [Toldot, also meaning "the story of"] *of Adam. In the day that God created man, in the likeness of God made He him; male and female He created them, and blessed them, and called their name Adam, in the day when they were created."* (Genesis 5:1-2)

These brief verses remind us of some very important ideas related to mankind and its story:

The first human was created as one unified being.

This being, called Adam, was both male and female.

This unified being, containing within it all contradictions, is in the likeness or image of God.

This single, unified being which contains contradictions is blessed!

And it is the pursuit of this blessing that is described in Parashat Toldot.

Right from the beginning it is clear that every offspring of Adam seeks to be blessed. One could say that the entire Torah deals with this one single idea: blessing. God blesses the first human; ten generations later He blesses Noach after the Flood; ten generations after that He blesses Avraham. This last blessing contains an entirely new element: You, Avraham, will **be** a blessing. It is your task to spread blessing in the world. You will teach people to be blessed, because that is their entirety.

It seems we are all blessed, but much to our dismay, we do not know it.

How many of us live our lives genuinely feeling that we are blessed?

It is because we lack a sense of being blessed that we long for the blessing of our Heavenly and earthly parents.

It is no coincidence that the story of Toldot describes a race for a blessing. Yitzchak, who is now blind, wants to bless Eisav, his beloved firstborn. He sends Eisav to hunt food and prepare his favorite dishes for him, after which Yitzchak will bless him. Rivka, who thinks there is only one blessing to be had, calls Yaakov, *her* beloved son, and arranges for him to bring his father the food which will earn him the blessing, thereby bypassing his brother.

From the moment of this deception everything goes wrong. Eisav, sorely disappointed, asks his father in great pain: Do you have only one blessing in your heart? And the truth is that Yitzchak has two blessings – one for each son. But he has given the one meant for Eisav to Yaakov, who will spend the next twenty years hiding from his brother's wrath, but also from his brother's blessing.

Rivka's punishment for the deception is that she will never again see her beloved Yaakov, and one assumes that Eisav is lost to her as well.

Yaakov and Eisav are twins, born from the same womb; one hairy and one smooth, one a hunter and the other a tent dweller; one a mama's boy and the other a papa's boy; one wild and the other תם (sorry, no good translation found for this beautiful word…, but read on).

The root of the word for twins is ת.א.מ. These are the last, the first and the middle letters of the alphabet. This signifies completeness, the completeness found when opposing sets become one, and this happens throughout the Bible: darkness and light, heaven and earth, land and sea, day and night, male and female, Cain and Hevel, (the Tree of Knowledge of-) Good and Evil. There are even two stories of Creation, with two different names for the Creator. In the first, Adam is created both male and female by Elohim, in His likeness. In the second, Adonai Elohim creates Man from the dust of the earth.

Later on in the Bible there are other dramas to do with the number two: Yishmael and Yitzchak, Eisav and Yaakov, Leah and Rachel, Yoseph and his brothers, Yoseph's two sons Ephraim and Menashe, Moshe and Aharon. Yaakov has two names: Yaakov, given by his parents, and Israel given by his blessing.

And then, at Mount Sinai, we see that the Torah is also given in twos: two tablets, two sets of tablets – one heavenly and one earthly. Two kinds of mitzvot – mitzvot of action and mitzvot of abstention; also, mitzvot between people and those between man and God. On their way to the Promised Land, Bnei Yisrael carry two arks – one with the two sets of Tablets, and the other with the bones of Yoseph.

All of Creation centers on the principle of duality – everything that *is*, all of Creation, comes in twos.

This is the source of primal human anguish. It is the pain of separation between what is me and all that is not me. When God separates male from female he casts deep sleep upon Adam. The text never relates that Adam awoke from that sleep.

Hence, duality may be viewed as unconsciousness, and unity as the state of awareness.

It is no coincidence that only from the birth of Yaakov do we begin to read about dreams in the Torah. Both Yaakov and his beloved son Yoseph dream big dreams. The dreams, too, come in sets of two: Yaakov dreams of angels going up and down a ladder connecting heaven and earth. As a child, Yoseph dreams two dreams in which his brothers submit to him. Years later, he dreams two dreams in an Egyptian prison about the plight of the baker and the plight of the steward. He is then brought before Pharaoh to interpret his two dreams - those of the years of plenty and those of drought.

Yaakov is our father. He is us. We are all enveloped in a deep sleep, dreaming nightmares about reality. Upon meeting Pharaoh before his death, Yaakov tells the king that his life has been bad – that he has lived a nightmare of a life. (ער means "awake" and רע means "bad" - the same letters in reverse order.)

Yaakov epitomizes the sleeping person who has nightmares. When confronting his stunned brothers in Egypt Yoseph asks them: Is our father alive?, meaning: Does our father still have nightmares or has he awakened and begun to live?

Yaakov's world is full of perceived injustice:

- Father loves my brother more and accepts his gifts
- My brother is older, stronger, and bigger. I am small and weak.
- I am smarter, so if I have used my brains to get his birthright, why does Father still want to give the blessing to my brother?

41

- I didn't steal his birthright – he sold it to me! It's mine fair and square, so why should he want to hurt me and why do I have to escape from him?
- Besides, it was all Mother's idea, not mine.
- None of this is fair!! The world isn't fair!

Yaakov's nightmare is our reality. There is me and there is the other. (In Yaakov's case, his brother.)

And we, the descendants of Yaakov, look at our history and see that while it was glorious, it was also hard and sometimes even bad, at times no less than a nightmare! 4,000 years later it continues to be challenging, and often we feel like yelling: it's not fair!

So what nightmare are we hoping to awaken from, and how can it be done?

That we will find out in two weeks' time. Two Parashot from now there will be beautiful closure, a new dawn in which Yaakov will "awaken" from his nightmare, and reunite with his twin. Only then, when Yaakov struggles with God and becomes Israel, will the damage caused by the stolen blessing be repaired.

What is two weeks compared to Jewish eternity…? However, you/we don't have to wait that long. The blessing that Yaakov is seeking, the blessing that we are all seeking, is not in heaven, nor is it "out there", in the distance, in our brothers' possession.

It is right here. Ever so close. Waiting for us to wake up; patiently waiting to be recognized. We are all blessed; we just don't seem to know it.

Parashat Vayetzeh: The Healing Power of the Truth

Is it possible to overcome anger?

Is it possible to hasten forgiveness?

Is it possible to bring about reconciliation and peace?

In Parashat Vayetzeh Yaakov begins a 20-year exile. He kisses his parents goodbye and escapes quickly from his twin brother's wrath. He does not yet know that he will never again see his mother, a very heavy price to pay for a stolen blessing.

While in exile he marries twice, has children with four different women, learns to out-maneuver his father-in-law's wiliness and becomes very wealthy. But all of the wealth, the children, and the deceptions do not make up for the pain he has left behind. They do not prevent the longing for his homeland, for his aging parents, even for his twin brother. All of his achievements do not silence his existential angst.

Is it possible to reduce his pain?

The poet of The Song of Songs says not – it is not possible to hasten processes: *"...awaken not, nor stir up love, until it please."* (Song of Songs 2:7) Tradition attributes to the same author the verse *"To every thing there is a season, and a time to every purpose under the heaven..."* (Ecclesiastes 3:1)

In other words, a higher wisdom tells us that everything happens in its time. Processes have their own rhythms which must be played out, and the timing of the process is also beneficial to the outcome.

This week Yaakov pays the price for his previous actions. First of all, he pays for the notion that the rights of the firstborn can be purchased – for money or for red lentils. He also pays for tricking his father and stealing his brother's blessing.

Our Sages try valiantly to clear Yaakov's reputation. They describe Eisav as a villain whose blessing needs to be reassigned. Later on in the story the deception is attributed to Rivka. But it doesn't matter! Unpardonable actions took place, and excuses do not exonerate Yaakov from the full weight of punishment. In previous drashot we have written about the idea of "it's not fair" being unproductive and detached from reality. Every action – good and less good - has consequences and price. This week we see a case in point.

But this week we also ask a very Yaakov-like question: is it possible to bargain about the results and the cost? Is it possible to sweeten the blow of punishment? Or, to paraphrase the poet: can love be awakened before its time?

Recuperation from physical harm is bound by laws of physics, biology and chemistry. A good ointment may hasten healing, and this is easily measurable. But what about emotional harm? Each kind of emotion has its own strength and current, and these alter between people as well. There are those who find it easy to truly forgive and move on, and others who will take any slight with them to the grave and beyond, if possible.

This indicates that there is something very subjective about the process of emotional healing. If this is the case, then perhaps it *is* possible to hasten it! On the other hand – why hasten? If we look at Yaakov's life, we see that the period in which he is in exile is very good. He marries, has children, and succeeds professionally. He also has time and distance to dispel the fear with which he escaped his country and to consider how best to return.

The period of healing and pardoning may be very valuable. If it had been rushed, perhaps Yaakov would not have been ready for the transition (which takes place next week) into Israel, and there would *be* no Israel.

Still (and I'm not trying to rush the process…) – is there a way to shorten the period of anger, fear, hurt and jealousy? Do we have to spend valuable time in our precious, not-so-long lives filled with such negative feelings?

I think not! I think it is possible to shorten the period of healing and to awaken love. How? It's really very simple, and also very difficult!

The only way I know how to do this is with the truth. Truth heals! But as we all know very well, we all lie. Not intentionally, and not because we intend to. We are simply blind to entire parts of our existence. We deny that which is dark, that which causes pain, and we try to look good in our own eyes and in the eyes of others. In order to face the truth two things are needed: a fierce desire for the truth, whatever the cost, and a good friend. Sometimes that person can be a caregiver, a coach, or just a passing stranger with the right comment at the right time. Any of these people might help us discover in what ways we lie to ourselves, and help us find the healing truth.

In my humble opinion, the truth may be found where blame ends. Any kind of blame is always a kind of escape from the truth. Blame seeks justice, not truth. Regardless of whether we are blaming ourselves or others, it has no connection to the truth, because all it does is drown us or others in a sense of guilt and sheds no light on what is or isn't true.

Yaakov will learn this next week. He will try to bribe Eisav with gifts, and Eisav will not have them. The "fact" is, that the minute Eisav sees that Yaakov has truly undergone a deep transformation, 20 years of anger will dissolve. What matters is not bribery, but truth. And the truth is also that every truth has a deeper truth hiding beneath it. Forever. In other words, even when Yaakov learns the lesson of his life, there will be other new and difficult lessons to be learned about the nature of truth. It is a lifelong pursuit for all of us.

I love Yaakov –he touches my heart. I love the illusion of weakness and threat that he feels his entire life, even though he is actually the strong one in the story. I love the way he truly understands that he has to pay the price of his actions. I love the way he bears the reality of his life. I love his helplessness in relation to Laban, to Rachel's barrenness, to Levi and Shimon's violence, and in relation to Eisav. Yaakov never claims that it isn't fair. Eisav is actually the one who cries out in pain: "Father, it's not fair! I hate him! I will kill my brother!" I truly feel for Eisav, but…

Yaakov and not Eisav is the one who is worthy of being called Israel, just as later, it will be Yehuda and not Reuven or Yoseph, who will be worthy of being the father of the Jewish (Yehudi) nation.

This week we go into exile with Yaakov. We agree to pay the price of our actions. We stop arguing with what is true, we stop blaming ourselves and others. We acknowledge our lot and continue to labor to build our world. In this way we can reduce the length of our suffering and hasten reconciliation.

Looking for blame may provide some comfort in the form of justice and vengeance, but not a sense of reconciliation.

Parashat Vayishlach: The Answer is in the Name

To all of our American olim, happy Thanksgiving. We, the natives of THIS country (Israel), want to thank you for being part of this amazing journey, of building a vibrant pluralistic community in our homeland. And now, the drasha, which has direct bearing on the subject!

Have we perhaps misunderstood the meaning of our nation's name?

In this week's parasha, Vayishlach, Yaakov becomes Israel. This is the first time that the name appears in the Torah, and I have a feeling that we accept its meaning at face value rather than looking deeper.

Interpreters have wondered why the Torah continues to use the name Yaakov, as well as the new name, Israel, after this story. When Avram becomes Avraham it is final. The same is true with Sarai becoming Sarah. Why not in Yaakov's/Israel's case?

Here is what the text relates, just as Yaakov sees Eisav's welcome committee. Yaakov turns to God and prays:

"*'O God of my father Avraham, and God of my father Yitzchak, O LORD, who said to me: Return to your country, and to your kindred, and I will do you good; I am not worthy of all the mercies, and of all the truth, which You have shown unto Your servant; for with my staff I passed over this Jordan; and now I am become two camps. Deliver me, I pray You, from the hand of my brother, from the hand of Eisav; for I fear him, lest he come and smite me, the mother with the children. And You said: I will surely do you good, and make your seed as the sand of the sea, which cannot be numbered for multitude.'*" (Bereishit 32:10-13) These words have been put to music in recent years in the very popular song, "קטנתי" by Yehonatan Razel.

Yaakov then sends his family across the Jordan and he stays behind:

"And Yaakov was left alone; and there a man wrestled with him until the breaking of the day. And when he [who?] *saw that he prevailed not against him, he touched the hollow of his thigh; and the hollow of Yaakov's thigh was strained, as he wrestled with him. And he* [who?] *said: 'Let me go, for the day breaks.' And he* [who?] *said: 'I will not let you go, unless you bless me.' And he said unto him: 'What is your name?' And he said: 'Yaakov.' And he said: 'Your name shall be called no more Yaakov, but Israel; **for you have struggled with God and with men**, and have prevailed.' And Yaakov asked him, and said: 'Tell me, I pray you, your name.' And he said: Why do you ask after my name?' And he blessed him there. And Yaakov called the name of the place P'niel: 'for I have seen God face to face, and my life is preserved.' "*(25-31) Then Yaakov crosses the Jordan, joins his family and faces his brother, upon which: *"Eisav ran to meet him, and embraced him, and fell on his neck, and kissed him; and they wept."*

The premise of this entire passage is based on the traditional reading of the words "Sarita im", as "you have struggled with". In Hebrew, the verb "struggle" should be followed by the word "against" not "with". The use of the "with" here implies the use of a tool or an aid, such as fighting with sticks and stones.

Therefore, I want to suggest a different reading, one that changes the entire picture, and with it the understanding of the name of our nation and its purpose. The key to this reading begins earlier, with the description of Yaakov's struggle **with** the mysterious man in the night, and later, in the words "for you have struggled **with** God and **with** men".

48

The implication is that there is some kind of unification here between God who struggles (Yisra-El) and Yaakov who struggles. Somehow, at least for a brief interval in the night, Yaakov ceases to be the scared, fearful refugee, and senses oneness with God. Yaakov feels that he has God with him, through him, for him, in him.

This feeling, as bizarre as it may sound, is there for the taking if one works at it. It is there in the powerful, fleeting moments of our lives when we cease being our confined individual selves and become one with Creation, with God. I do not mean this in the sense of personal grandeur. On the contrary – our sense of self makes way for all existence and we are small and humble in comparison.

In my opinion, the real fall from grace in the Garden of Eden was that after eating from the Tree of Knowledge we identified ourselves as specific, finite individuals rather than an integral part of Creation. To this day, we are in exile from that ultimate mode of being.

Yaakov, who is scared and fearful of what the meeting with his brother will bring, stays alone in the dark night and experiences complete solitude. But he is not alone; he is with a man **with** whom he struggles, not against. Yaakov finally realizes that he is never really alone, that God (or his angel, i.e. the man) is always there waiting to flow with and through him. Throughout his life, Yaakov has been so busy being fearful and directing his life that he has never discovered this, just as happens in our own lives.

This may be why the Torah leaves the conversation between Yaakov and the man so unclear in terms of who is addressing whom. Yaakov does not get an answer to his request "Tell me your name," because there is no name to tell – the man and Yaakov are one and the same. This is why Yaakov is blessed and why he says he saw God face to face. He has experienced that divine sense of oneness.

Although the sun comes up and Yaakov recedes into his individual identity (and to his previous name), he retains an impression of his experience as he goes to greet his brother, realizing that they, too, are one and always have been. Throughout the rest of his life, Yaakov will be called thus when limited and fearful, and Israel in moments of greatness, when he senses himself as part of God in the world.

Parashat Vayeshev:
A Path Strewn with "Klipot" of Pain

Imagine a deep, comfortable easy-chair in the yard, under an ancient oak tree on a pleasant summer day in the Judean hills. An old man gazes out at the view. He sees his (genetically-engineered) flock, and his grown sons herding on the foothills. He has had many difficulties with them. Just recently he himself has made peace with his twin brother, the wild redhead. Now it is their turn to bicker. Why doesn't anyone learn from their parents' experience, he wonders. He glances lovingly at his favorite son who is napping nearby. The boy's eyelids move rapidly, as if dreaming wild and exciting dreams of wheat and stars. Behind him he hears the sound of his youngest son crying. Just a baby and already being taken care of by women who didn't much like his late mother. Every cry reminds him of his great love who died because of his hasty vow that whoever stole Lavan's idols will die. He sighs.

Parashat Vayeshev might have related a happy ending to the complicated story of Yaakov's life and adventures, having returned from twenty years of exile. All he wants to do is sit quietly under the oak tree. But there are other plans in store for him. In just a few verses, his beloved son Yoseph will be sold by his brothers to a convoy of travelling Yishmaelite merchants. As Yoseph is led as merchandise to the slave market in Egypt, his brothers approach their father with a striped coat covered in blood. Yaakov descends into a world of pain and sorrow.

Meanwhile, in Egypt, Yoseph's luck turns once when he is sold to a high-ranking official, and again when he is accused of attempted rape and he is thrown into an Egyptian prison.

This parasha contains so much pain, jealousy, cruelty, and heartache! The brothers' actions reflect our own, as always. We prefer to look into a mirror to put on makeup, to improve our image and hide our faults. This week, together with Yoseph, we will face them, literally.

But we must do so with great care! The goal is not to judge ourselves harshly, and to remember that under our protective layers of makeup and clothes our skin is very tender.

The jealousy that causes Yoseph's brothers to act as they do is the same jealousy that exists between Cain and Hevel, Yitzchak and Yishmael, Eisav and Yaakov, Rachel and Leah; and us, of course. Jealousy wreaks havoc on humanity each and every day. In a way, we are all siblings with the same evolutionary, spiritual or symbolic parent, and we all vie for that parent's affection and grace. We are consumed by jealousy every time we feel that another person has been favored more than us.

From Cain and until this very day the same jealousy exists —nothing has changed. Revolutions have come and gone, the world has been destroyed by wars, and still jealousy rages on. There is always a "sibling" who has more than we do – a higher IQ or salary, more obvious talent, better verbal skills, better looking, more virtual or real friends. There is always something to be jealous of and there always will be.

There is only one way that I know of to release ourselves from jealousy, and it is to make a radical distinction, one that we are never taught to make, between essence and shell, called "klippa" in Jewish mysticism.

Everything is a klippa. Every thing, every object is a klippa. There is no thing that is not a klippa. People are distinct from one another and from objects based on their klippa because this is all we see, hear, and touch. Therefore, jealousy is only at the level of the klippa, the external. Klipot are definitely important, but essence is much more so.

It is difficult to discuss essence, because as soon as we turn it into words we are creating klipot –external manifestations. Nonetheless, I will try to offer a few images, because these are all we have for this purpose. Essence is the Divine energy that enables Creation. It is all of the klipot together. In the Torah, the essence is the light of the first day of Creation, the light that existed before the sun was created on the fourth day. This primal light was hidden at the creation of Man. It was hidden –so say our Sages – for use by the righteous ones sometime in the future. Who are those righteous ones? They are those who will recognize the primal, eternal light that is hidden behind every klippa, the light that enables and gives life to every klippa.

Reuven, Shimon, Levi, Yehuda, Yoseph, Benyamin... these are some of the infinite klipot of that same hidden light. Each klippa looks at the other and sees... a klippa. Not light, not essence, not God. Just a klippa. In the realm of klipot there is always a more beautiful, more popular, more "successful", and definitely a more threatening one than our own.

We are now in the last, darkest part of the month of Kislev, the darkest days of the year. This is exactly when we celebrate Chanuka, lighting an additional candle each night. But we are not meant to use these candles for light or warmth; not even to perform the mitzvah itself! Only to witness the light. This is because using it turns it into a thing, a klippa. The miracle of Chanuka can be seen only when one really looks inside and witnesses the great miracle of the essence, a glimpse of the hidden primal light.

The laws of candle lighting instruct us to place all of the candles at the same level in order to remind us that there is no difference between them, just as there is no difference between people. This is not a PC statement but a statement of truth, of essence. While it is true that each person is unique, this is only at the level of klippa, where each has a role and a place. Our essence, however, is One; it is Eternal; it is Infinite.

Yoseph is called "Yoseph the righteous one". The righteous are in awe of the klippa but do not take it seriously. It may take the form of a coat of many colors or the rags of a slave; it may look like the suit of a butler or the uniform of a prisoner. It may even look like the outfit of the king's assistant. This is why Yoseph dons and discards each of these in turn, and the hidden light does not change.

Just as in Yoseph's dreams the sheaves of wheat bow down and acknowledge the light of Creation, and the stars owe their light to the same Source, so it is with many of our dreams: they may come true, but they may also leave klipot of pain in their wake.

Shabbat Shalom and a Happy Festival of Lights

Chanuka & Miketz – It's a Miracle... Isn't It?

This week we read about Yoseph – how he rots in jail although innocent of charges against him; how, after many years, he is set free and becomes an important figure in Pharaoh's court. Is this a miracle? Is it a dream come true?

Let us consider this further. Who can compensate him for the lost years? Can Yoseph overcome the trauma of separation from his father and the actions of his brothers just because he becomes second to the king? Can he truly feel set free? Is it by chance or by choice that he does not visit his father during his years of privilege, when he is able to do so? Why does Yoseph choose to adopt an Egyptian identity and name, so that even his brothers don't recognize him, although he is able to recognize them?

Cut to the Maccabees, 2,180 years later. They won the battle and purified the Temple, but what all about those fine fighters who did not make it home to celebrate? This is true of all of Israel's battles: there are those who never make it to the final, emotional finish. Some families get to hold their returning loved one while others must continue living although their lives have fallen apart.

Can there be a victory that is all sweetness and no scars? What, exactly, constitutes a miracle in this context?

I read a wonderful explanation by the Israeli singer-songwriter, Yuval Dor. He said that a miracle is something which is held or holds aloft; just as a flag does (the word for flag in Hebrew is the same as the word for "miracle" – "ness"). A flag, like a miracle, causes us to raise our eyes above the mundane. A miracle is not an occurrence that is elevated above us physically. Rather, it is above and beyond the natural order. Nature is neither good nor bad, nor does it have memory or meaning of its own. Flags and miracles certainly do.

Let us examine, then, what is miraculous about Chanuka and Parashat Miketz. Pharaoh dreams and Yoseph's talent for interpreting dreams gets him out of prison and sends him off to stardom. No miracle there. The Maccabees, native to the mountainous region, use impressive mountain tactics and strategy to win their war. These are not miracles. They are a natural cause and effect.

The miracles appear when the young Yoseph is able to find meaning in his difficult destiny, to avoid despair, and keep his eyes on the greater vision. Miracles appear when a small band of dedicated fighters are able to tap unbelievable hidden resources. These are beyond the natural way of the world, and therefore miraculous.

Since the time of the Sages, we tell our children that the miracle of Chanuka lies in the cute story of the little tin of oil. That is divine magic, at best, not a miracle. So too, Yoseph's miracle is not the magical fulfillment of his dreams but rather the story of his spirit, which is never broken, even in the darkest of pits.

These kinds of miracles happen constantly. They happen any time inner strength lifts us above the banality of routine, of thought-less nature, of the endless cycle of birth, life and death. Whenever the human spirit exercises its ability to make free choices, to lift, move, wave, and direct our lives, a miracle occurs.

No wonder the Maccabean story sparked the imagination and awe of the early Zionists. Zionism, the State of Israel, and all that has happened here since then, are contrary to the "natural order". The entire story of this "start-up nation" is authored by people who elevated their gaze beyond the death pits of Europe, to a vision that changed the history of the Jewish People.

Interestingly enough, the early pioneers declared in a song that every Israeli child knows by heart: "A miracle never happened to us. We never found a tin of oil. We descended to the valleys. We ascended up the mountain. Hidden springs of light we discovered… We chiseled the rock until there was blood. And behold, there was light."

This song was written many years ago. Is the spirit of the miraculous still here?

A very popular, more current, Israeli song, written by Micha Sheetrit and Leah Shabbat, suggest that while it the Israeli spirit may have changed, or even been transformed, it is nevertheless still the heartbeat of the Israeli psyche.

Whatever happens I will make a difference
I will fulfill my dream
Those who bear bad tidings, plagues or decrees
Will not change my essence.

You and I and the God that is with us
Will be victorious
Not through power
But through the spirit
That blows from behind.
Only because of the spirit inside me - in my mind, in my soul.
Only because of the spirit
In me - in my blood, in my soul.

I will shout what I have to say
So that it will be heard even on the moon
I will not forget

Those who say "not so"
A day will come when I will prove I was right.

You and I and the God that is with us....

Happy Chanuka and Shabbat Shalom

Parashat Vayigash: The Art of Approaching

This week we learn how to approach - Vayigash or Lageshet in Hebrew.

Many years have passed since Yaakov's sons threw their brother into the pit. Yehuda, who seemed to be the leader of the pack, now approaches the advisor to the king of Egypt and begs him to take him as hostage instead of Benyamin. Yoseph, who has already recognized his distressed brothers months ago, has been testing or teasing them; perhaps he is taking revenge, or maybe he is setting the stage for the fulfillment of his childhood dreams in which each of his brothers bows down to him.

He is moved when he discovers that his brothers have looked out for Benyamin and that they continue to do so. The same Yehuda who did not heed Yoseph's youthful plea for mercy, is now a mature, responsible man who is willing to forgo his own liberty for his brother's freedom and for the benefit of his father who cannot bear to lose another son, certainly not the second son of his beloved wife, Rachel.

Yehuda **approaches** and delivers a brilliant speech. It is impossible to resist his plea. Yoseph tries to resist but cannot. You can read the entire speech (Bereishit, Chapter 44) for the details. Our concern is with one word: to approach – "lageshet" (לגשת).

Following Yehuda's approach, we witness one of the most moving moments in the Torah. Yoseph breaks down, and his tears wash away the Egyptian mask behind which he has been hiding from his brothers.

"Then Yoseph could not refrain... And there stood no man with him, while Yoseph made himself known unto his brothers. And he wept aloud... And Yoseph said to his brothers: 'I am Yoseph; is my father still alive?'... And Yoseph said to his brothers: **'Come near to me,** *I pray you.' And they* **came near.** *And he said: 'I am Yoseph your brother, whom you sold into Egypt."* (Bereishit 45: 1-4)

Yehuda **approaches** Yoseph and pours out his heart. Yoseph calls his brothers to **come near (approach)** him and they **approach.** This is the essence of Parashat Vayigash: if one **approaches** correctly, the door opens. Everything depends on one's **approach** – how one comes near, and **approaches** one's fellow man or woman.

But what does approaching or "lageshet" mean?

The last time this word appeared was in the context of Yaakov's emotional reunion with his brother, Eisav. *"And Yaakov lifted up his eyes and looked, and, behold, Eisav came, and with him four hundred men... And he himself passed over before them, and bowed himself to the ground seven times, until he* **came near** *to his brother. And Eisav ran to meet him, and embraced him, and fell on his neck, and kissed him; and they wept... Then the handmaids* **came near,** *they and their children, and they bowed down. And Leah also and her children* **came near,** *and bowed down; and after* **came Yoseph near and Rachel,** *and they bowed down."* (Bereishit 33: 1-7)

One of the next times we will meet the same verb will be at Mount Sinai. A moment after the great revelation, the people are standing scared and anxious. God invites them to an intimate encounter the likes of which has never been experienced. They find it difficult to accept this invitation, but Moshe does not hesitate. *"And the people stood afar off; but Moshe* **drew near** *unto the thick darkness where God was."* (Exodus 20:17)

This, then, is the point! Approaching is not a physical act. It is taking a risk, coming close to the thick darkness or fog, to the unknown, because this is where God is to be found: in the unknown.

It is easy to approach what is known and secure. One who thirsts for contact, for intimacy, for God (in the form of love) must agree to take the frightening leap into the unknown.

Yehuda does not know how the king's advisor will respond to his plea. It is reasonable to assume that the advisor might harm him. Yaakov also does not know how Eisav will react. God has not promised him a loving reception. Eisav has a company of 400 men behind him, probably bearing arms. Yoseph beckons his brothers to approach him, but he doesn't say "all is well, have no fear". He just says "approach". This is a very difficult request!

Approach love; approach that which you have been pining for for years – your brother, your God. Face your mistakes; make peace in your heart.

I don't have a formula for how this is done. The Torah gives us broad guidelines which provide direction and intent:

The direction is towards the other, your brother who is also your mirror: Ya'akov and Eisav, Yoseph and his brothers, Moshe and HaShem.

The intent is your longing, the love that is hiding under layers of jealousy, fear and hatred. That love is always there.

This is really the essence of Bereishit. It is a book that calls upon us to approach.

Sh'mot will soon begin, and teach us another word: Bo. Stay tuned…

Parashat Vayechi: The Secret of Parallel Lives

This week we take leave of Bereishit, of Yaakov, Yoseph and all of that amazing, complicated generation. Yaakov blesses his sons, and in doing so gives us a clue to the key that can take us out of Egypt.

"And Yaakov lived in the land of Egypt seventeen years; so the days of Yaakov, the years of his life, were a hundred forty and seven years."(Bereishit 47: 28)

The "years of his life" is written in a more ambiguous way in Hebrew, and it can also be read as "his two lives". When the summarizing verse of a biblical person's life is thus worded, our Sages tell us that the intention is to describe two parts of that person's life. In Yaakov's case, the reference is to his life prior to and after being reunited with his beloved son Yoseph.

The first chapter of Yaakov's life involves a very long wait for the birth of a child of his beloved, barren wife, who then dies giving birth to their second son. That first, long-awaited child is taken away from him at the age of 17 and exiled to Egypt.

The second chapter - that of reunion - takes place on foreign soil. This chapter is also 17 years long – 17 years of forgiveness, blessing, abundance and comfort – until Yaakov dies in the fullness of years, in the presence of his beloved son.

These are two chapters of Yaakov's life. But there are other ways we can divide his life into two chapters:

- Before and after stealing his brother's blessing from their father.

- Before becoming Israel and after the nighttime struggle with the angel.
- And there are more…

Every person has at least two lives, not necessarily divided into chronological chapters; in fact they often overlap. Here are some examples of the ways in which our lives may be divided:

- Our inner, chaotic world, and the external one, which generally looks reasonably intact.
- Our subjective and often distorted view of our lives, and the objective, "real" perspective.
- Our heart and our mind.

We live our lives with all kinds of assumptions, thoughts, beliefs and perceptions that may or may not have any connection to the deep, inner truth of our lives. It is not that we are liars… well, perhaps we are, just a little… and sometimes a lot – but usually quite unintentionally.

Mostly we are blind or we are in denial. We truly believe that we know a thing or two about ourselves, only to discover in old age - as Socrates said - that we know nothing.

In a moment of chilling honesty on the occasion of his meeting with Pharaoh, Yaakov says: *'...few and evil have been the days of the years of my (two) lives...'* (47:9)

I won't discuss "few and evil" at this point, but it can certainly be said about Yaakov that he lives most of his life in darkness of one kind or another. Each time darkness prevails, it is the result of some kind of deception or escape:

1. His mother, who knows something he does not, causes him to steal his brother's blessing.
2. His brother wants to kill him, making it unclear if and when Yaakov can return home.
3. A beloved bride is replaced cunningly with her sister under the chuppah.
4. His fears of his father-in-law, Lavan, may not allow him to return to his home with his family and possessions.
5. The oath he swears against whoever stole the idols, destining his beloved wife to an early death in childbirth.
6. The kidnapping and rape of his only daughter, Dinah.
7. The actions of his sons Shimon and Levi as a result of that rape – slaughtering the people of Sh'chem after Yaakov makes an agreement with them.
8. His blind preference of Yoseph over all of his other children, which causes tremendous jealousy and tragedy.
9. The deadly errand on which he unwittingly sends Yoseph.
10. The great sadness he experiences believing his beloved son dead, unable to find comfort throughout the years during which Yoseph is alive and successful in a neighboring country.

We live our lives on two levels – seen and unseen, explicit and implicit. We think we know, understand, and comprehend. We think we have a clue as to causes and their effects. But the truth (maybe) is that we have no idea. The most we can do is hold on to reasonable assumptions. Even the laws of gravity can only be observed, never fully proven. All of science is based on repeated results of experiments and observations. All we can say is that the same result was attained. We cannot prove beyond doubt that it will necessarily happen again.

I am not a fatalist. I am always in search of a redemptive prospect. I would like to understand, then - what is redeeming about this notion?

This Shabbat we will finish reading Bereishit. We have arrived in the Egyptian fleshpots, where food is abundant. We are happy, and we're going to stay in Egypt for a long time. Pharaoh will die and a new king will arise who will not remember all that Yoseph did for Egypt. There is a fairly good chance that our emigration to Egypt will end in slavery.

Will we remember our way back? Will we know how to leave the fleshpots and return home?

The only enslavement I know of (there could, of course, be more) is that of empirical knowledge. It is fine to live our lives and make assumptions based on our ongoing observations. We need assumptions in order to maintain our sanity. But great freedom is to be had when we accept that we have no idea how things really happen; that indeed, anything can happen. Everything is possible.

So just before the generations of slavery appear next week, Yaakov hands us the key to our freedom, to our redemption: there is never one view of life. There may be one visible right now, yet all options are open. If only one road seems apparent, slavery and oppression have taken hold.

May we be open to this possibility, and to others – endless others.

After all, why limit ourselves?

Parashat Sh'mot: Who am "I"?

This week our story takes a dramatic turn. Bnei Yisrael fall from the heights of glory to the depths of despair.

Conventional thought has it that the enslavement is the result of fear. Pharaoh feels threatened by the increasing power of Bnei Yisrael and so he takes steps to limit it. When this doesn't work he tries oppression – he attempts to dampen their will to live and to multiply. When this, too, doesn't work (quite to the contrary, as usual) he moves on to infanticide.

Conventional thought blames Pharaoh and paints Am Yisrael as the victim.

Yet according to classic Rabbinic thought Pharaoh is not to blame. He is just a pawn doing God's will: God uses Pharaoh to show His greatness in the world. This approach actually makes Pharaoh the victim! It would have suited Pharaoh's needs to be rid of the Israelite threat. He might have even encouraged them to leave, but God hardens his heart and does not allow it. And then abuse begins in the form of the plagues that God brings on Pharaoh and his people. God wants everyone – especially His Chosen People - to know that He is God and there is no other. Bnei Yisrael fail to remember their God and require a dramatic wake-up call. In that sense (and that sense only) they are responsible for what is happening.

This year I would like to go down another path altogether. The Hassidic, or rather the neo-Hassidic, approach addresses questions of slavery, descent and redemption in an entirely different way. In the psycho-Hassidic world, all parts of this great drama are parts within us, rendering the division of "us" and "them" an artificial one.

Before we continue with this line of thinking, I want to stress that while the parts exist within us, they are not necessarily US, not necessarily part of our "I", of who we are.

The Exodus story, in the neo-Hassidic approach, is a personal, inner, existential story. Hence we are told that "each person must see him or herself as having left Egypt".

Let us meet the characters of this inner drama.

1. Pharaoh is the false king whom we allow to take the throne. He reigns by generating fear. (This Pharaoh is "The son of the maiden who replaced the son of the King", from Rabbi Nachman's famous tale, "The Exchanged Children".) His way is to degrade and enslave others.
2. The brave midwives are the part of us that is committed to life. Their role is to bring forth, to give birth to life in the deepest sense of the word.
3. Amram and Yocheved, both Levites, represent the awareness of tradition and continuity within us. A Levite is proud and protective of his inherited identity. He will not allow anyone to abuse his beloved sister as we read in the story of Dina..
4. Speaking of the sister… The sister who watches the baby in his basket on the river has the quality of compassion and caring. Amram and Yocheved can be seen as a vertical connection to previous generations, whereas Miriam represents the horizontal connection between people, between family.
5. Pharaoh's daughter is the quality of justice, ethics, and conscience. She is the representative of the Divine Sh'china in human life. Our Sages call her "Batya"- the daughter of God.

6. The Egyptian man who beats the Israelite is the emissary of the false king. His job is to spread fear and oppression. He is the lethal voice of inner criticism.
7. Tzipporah (bird, in Hebrew) is the nest, the inner sanctum, the caring and supportive partner.
8. Yitro is the eyes; the responsible adult within us; the voice of practical wisdom. He teaches us how to organize our lives and bring harmony to all these inner parts.

Two very big questions remain:

1. What does Moshe represent?
2. When we look at all of these characters or qualities within us, who and where exactly is "I"?

Moshe is our complex existence. His speech is fragmented, and so is ours. He often gets angry and upset, and so do we. He would like to be left alone, but is called upon to fulfill a great variety of significant duties in his life. We too would often opt to go our own way, rather than take upon ourselves the huge burdens and responsibilities that life seems to want to place on our fragile shoulders.

Moshe's "I", with all of its complexities, is clear to see in the Torah. We, on the other hand, do not appear in the world so clearly characterized. In fact, what one sees when looking at us is quite the opposite. We appear scattered and undefined. Rarely is our "I" visible to the naked eye, though there are magical and memorable moments when it is.

I would like to suggest that the "I" in a person appears in full glory at the end of our parasha. It appears in the voice responding to Moshe at the burning bush, when Moshe asks "whom shall I say sent me"?

"'I will be what I will be'; and He said, Thus shall you say to the children of Israel: 'I Will Be' has sent me to you." (Exodus 3:14)

God says that this is the first time He has ever introduced Himself in this way. No one, until this parasha, ever asked "but wait, what does that mean?" (Note, this is not God's name. God's holy name will appear in the next Parasha, Parashat Ve'ara, as Y.H.V.H.). Moshe is the first to ask, and the first to be answered.

God's "Identity" is "I will be what I will be." And in short – "I Will Be", Eheye.

The expansive drama that begins with the descent of Bnei Yisrael to Egypt in search of food, through their huge success there and their eventual decline and slavery – is all part of the hidden story of Eheye; the invisible Divine "I".

The process of fulfillment and manifestation of a person's potential in the world is filled with the many characters of the Exodus story and their traits: the reign of the false "king", the "midwives" commitment to life; qualities of continuity, compassion, responsibility, justice, fear, criticism, quiet support, and wisdom. Throughout all of this, the invisible, Divine "I", Eheye, calls upon the visible human "I", Moshe, to free himself of falsehood, to go forth and become, to live.

This process happens daily. Jewish tradition recalls the Exodus story in our prayers and rituals several times throughout the day.

Rabbi Avraham HaCohen Kook, in one of his writings, explains this hidden "I", this way:

"Behold, I am in exile. The inner self, the inner "I" – the "I" of the individual and that of the collective… For we have all transgressed, along with our ancestors, the transgression of Adam, who estranged himself from his inner Self... He lost his Self, he did not know how to respond clearly to the question: "Ayeka?" - Where are You? Because he had lost his Self, his true inner "I" was lost unto him as well...

Until today, that is. Moshe is the first to rediscover the lost quality with which one comes out of Egypt, emerges out of the old, out of the confines of false kings and his task masters, and emerges, and becomes. Eheye Asher Eheye. I will become.

Parashat Va'era: When Suffering Feels Good

There is so much wisdom in this week's parasha, but also a lot of difficulty.

The process of leaving Egypt is beginning to gain momentum. So far, Moshe's intervention has only caused conditions to worsen for Bnei Yisrael. And not only does Pharaoh laugh in Moshe's face, but Bnei Yisrael are not interested in leaving either!

We, the readers, are torn between God's lofty promise of things to come, and the difficult reality of slavery which is only deteriorating.

Moshe is in need of support, and here, for the first time, he hears the five redemptive verbs which strengthen the promise and raise his spirits. (They appear every year at our Seder table!)

*"...I am the LORD, and I will **bring you** out from under the burdens of the Egyptians, and I will **deliver you** from their bondage, and I will **redeem you** with an outstretched arm, and with great judgments; and I will **take you** to Me for a people, and I will be to you a God... And I will **bring you** in unto the land, which I lifted up My hand to give to Avraham, to Yitzchak, and to Yaakov..."'* (Exodus 6: 6-8)

Moshe is encouraged and ready to convey these new messages, but...

"And Moshe spoke so unto the children of Israel; but they hearkened not unto Moshe for impatience of spirit, and for cruel bondage."

How often do we see people complaining about their lot when the solution is waiting right in front of them, yet they cannot or refuse to see it?! How often does it happen to each of us that we are confused and in pain but cannot or are unable to hear of a solution? We tell ourselves that our situation is uniquely complicated, a special case, not to be understood or solved so easily. And then we remain in "Egypt", "impatient of spirit, and for cruel bondage."

Why do we do this? Why do we refuse solutions and choose to suffer? Maybe because we are not really suffering; that is, we are, very much, but we are also absolutely fine as we are.

An explanation frequently given is that Bnei Yisrael prefer the devil they know (Egypt) to the devil they don't know. But perhaps there is a different explanation, a very simple one: perhaps they simply prefer to suffer!

I hesitate greatly to make such a statement. There are people who are suffering terribly at this very moment, and who am I to say that they prefer suffering to other alternatives, so I proceed with great caution.

I would like to make an important distinction - between pain and suffering. They are not the same! Pain – be it physical or emotional – may be an objective reality. Suffering is a matter of interpretation.

The Exodus story relates that Bnei Yisrael really did groan and cry out. In other words – it really hurt!

"And it came to pass in the course of those many days that the king of Egypt died; and the children of Israel sighed by reason of the bondage, and they cried, and their cry came up unto God by reason of the bondage. And God heard their groaning, and God

72

remembered His covenant with Avraham, with Yitzchak, and with Yaakov."(Exodus 2:23-24)

Their pain is real and intense, yet when it comes right down to it, they choose to remain in distress. Holding on to pain turns it into suffering.

Why do we do it? What do we gain by it? Many, many things!

First and foremost, we gain attention. Yet, far more significantly, our suffering gives us an identity! I suffer, therefore I am.

Identity is formed by erecting a fence between "me" and all that is not "me". This is true of personal identity as well as group identity (where the fence is broader and the suffering is often on a much larger scale). Without separation there is no identity, but separation is also a source of suffering.

We are so sure that we truly want peace and quiet, to be left alone. Yet, let's be honest, our ancestors did not bequeath us such an identity. Peace and quiet are boring! Uniqueness is interesting. In fact, "interesting" means, in essence, different, unique, other.

If we give up suffering, what is left? Who would we be without it?

God, through Moshe, is beckoning Bnei Yisrael to leave their suffering behind, to leave the narrow confines of their existence. He will *"come down to deliver them out of the hand of the Egyptians (Mitsrayim = narrow), and bring them up out of that land unto a good land, large and wide…"* (Exodus 3:8).

What will enable them and us to forego our suffering? What will make them and us able to listen?

I think the answer provided in the parasha is: plagues, hardships, and many of them. We have to experience great hardship, and our suffering needs to be intensified before we are able to listen. This was true not only for the Egyptians, but for B'nai Yisrael too; perhaps mostly for B'nai Yisrael. We will only listen or see when our self-imposed, limited identity becomes too oppressive.

Yet this is a dangerous call! Jewish educators have been laboring for decades to deepen the sense of Jewish identity – i.e., our sense of separateness, uniqueness, perhaps even greatness. Identity-building, it turns out, is a holy and risky task. Issues of Jewish identity, at least in the West, began when the walls of the European ghettos opened in the 19th century, and Jews were allowed, and often encouraged, to integrate into the surrounding culture. An internal sense of ethnic/religious chosen-ness on the one hand, and surrounding anti-Semitism on the other hand, spared us the need to deal with identity and assimilation.

But this is precisely the problem with our educational endeavor. We offer only two options: ethnic and religious identity or assimilation.

The word that denotes personal identity comes in the form of one single letter in English: "I".

Three weeks from now, in Parashat Yitro, God will declare His presence at Mount Sinai. When He will utter the opening word of the Ten Commandments, He will use a unique form of the one letter word "I". In Hebrew, it is "Anochi". Throughout the Torah the word "Anochi" is used both by humans and by God, so it is clearly not reserved for God referring to Himself. Yet, "Anochi" carries a certain magic, a magic that is not present in the more common word for "I", "Ani". When one uses "Anochi", there is a sense of a higher and broader "I" speaking, even if the speaker is a person.

When we mortals use the more common word for "I" ("ani"), we are referring to a very narrow "I" – that of personal identity. God's "I", on the other hand, is all-inclusive. It is liberating from the confines of narrowness of Egypt. In fact, it may actually be the essence of liberty.

Could it be, then, that the difference between pain and suffering comes down to our sense of "I"? That the narrower our sense of "I" is, the more our pain turns into suffering? That the broader the "I", the more our suffering is reduced to "simple" pain?

This is not a Buddhist calling to eliminate the "I". Far from it! It is a Jewish calling to deepen – but not to narrow - our sense of "I". It is an invitation to "know" an "I" that is Divine; an "I" that is both 100% unique and personal, and 100% all encompassing.

So, are we ready to broaden our narrow confines? Are we ready to expand the boundaries of our individual and collective identities?

This is the question of the Book of Exodus.

Parashat Bo: Farewell, Egypt, and Thank you

This week's parasha, Bo, is considered the jewel in the crown, or perhaps even the crown itself. Or maybe it is the head on which the crown with the jewel rests. Rashi writes that the Torah should have begun with this parasha instead of "In the beginning..."

Jewish time begins with Parashat Bo: *"This month shall be unto you the beginning of months; it shall be the first month of the year to you."*(Exodus 12:2)

Am Yisrael is beginning to tell its story as a people and to leave its mark on the history of civilization. The connotation of the word "human" also changes, and comes to imply the right or even the obligation to be free.

Why can all of this be attributed to Bo? Because the Exodus begins here. It's that simple. Or is it?

Pharaoh has finally had enough – he sends Bnei Yisrael away like an "unwanted bride": *"And the LORD said unto Moshe: 'Yet one plague more will I bring upon Pharaoh* [the death of the firstborn son] *and upon Egypt; afterwards he will let you go hence as he would a bride, he shall surely thrust you out hence altogether."* (11:1)

This is the first and most publicized divorce in Jewish history. The Torah does not use words lightly; it is very precise. It appears that there was a very compatible relationship between Bnei Yisrael and Pharaoh, so much so that they are compared to a married couple. One wonders - were they ever "in love"? In any case, it's now over, and Pharaoh – like many divorcees – does not remember the good old days when Yoseph saved Egypt from starvation.

Divorce is a lengthy process, even when it is timely. Even with the scent of freedom in the air, separation takes time.

Pharaoh is the first to take a stand. If it was up to Bnei Yisrael, they might have stayed forever, as long as they were comfortable. But Pharaoh has caught them unaware – they have not realized that the charmed life is over, and it is time to leave. Why would they? Things have been going so well…

At first Pharaoh doesn't want to send Bnei Yisrael away, just to squeeze more labor out of them, to use their presence to the fullest. But didn't Bnei Yisrael do the same thing? Didn't they come to Egypt because they were hungry and wanted to better their circumstances? And then, when the drought ended, they could have returned home but didn't, because Egypt was useful to them.

Pharaoh is worried when he sees how comfortable Bnei Yisrael are and how they are multiplying and growing stronger, and he decides he's had enough; the mutually useful relationship must come to an end. He enslaves them, tortures them, and tries to obliterate them. Bnei Yisrael see it differently: as evil takes hold they are slow to respond. At first they adjust; then they get bitter and cry a bit. Then they cry a lot. Then they cry out but still don't understand what has to happen. Only when realization strikes do they consider going home, to the Land of Israel. Until that point, they are in shock, paralyzed by the new reality, hoping that it will all sort itself out.

By the time Bnei Yisrael want to leave, Pharaoh cannot let them go. Like a jealous husband filled with hatred and evil, he holds onto them and abuses them. Bnei Yisrael are the first to be denied a divorce. Finally, however, it is granted and this week the bride is sent away with her ketubah in hand: the silver and gold belonging to the Egyptian neighbors. (She has to steal them, but still...)

There are many lessons to be learned from this story:
- Couplehood that is based on mutual usefulness comes to an end when one side no longer finds it to be so.
- When one side wants out there is no point in holding on – when it's over it's over.
- Beyond interests and usefulness lies something more important: words like destiny, a place to call home, truth, and essence.
- It takes a lot of courage and honesty to uncover that which is hidden underneath utility and interest.

Usefulness will almost always trump more profound feelings because it is clever and wily and masquerades as love and great promise, even when it suffocates.

When one side or other is no longer interested in maintaining the relationship and the other is, it is painful, especially if that other side is in denial – continuing to confuse usefulness with love, truth, or essence.

This week that denial breaks down. Through great pain and dramatic plagues Bnei Yisrael understand that although there were a lot of good and useful experiences, it is time to go; to dig deeper into their (our) purpose and destiny.

Both Egypt and Bnei Yisrael have benefitted from the relationship. This is why Bnei Yisrael are warned later in their journey not to hate the Egyptians. They were strangers in their land, were given refuge there from the famine, and therefore owe a great debt of gratitude.

And perhaps one more important lesson, before we part and break up this utilitarian marriage: Not one moment was for naught! The entire experience of refuge-turned-slavery was important, but now it is time to say "Farewell, Egypt, and THANK YOU."

Parashat BeShalach:
Seeing the Abundance That Surrounds Us

70 years ago a miracle happened, a miracle which was no less significant than the ultimate, mythic miracle of the parting of the Red Sea. Perhaps it was even more miraculous: a broken, denigrated People returned home and founded a state.

This miracle did not happen in the United Nations on the 29th of November 1947. It happened in the years preceding and especially following this date. There was no time to wait for the dough to rise; no time to mourn the loss of near and dear, the cruel deaths of women and children, men and babies, grandmothers and grandfathers.

Just like this week's Torah portion, things closed in from all sides: armies, a world embargo, and there was no place to run to. A nation of persecuted refugees crossed deserts and seas, and breathtakingly changed its own destiny, an achievement that none of its predecessors had dared to achieve since Jewish independence ended in 135 C.E.

As in our parasha, one thing this People knew how to do well was sing: songs of redemption, of praise, of love, in the shadow of war, songs of longing for their old-new land, songs of the Land of Israel.

As in our parasha, only 70 years have passed since that miracle, and no one seems to remember or mention it. Our existence here in Israel is taken for granted, as if there has always been a Jewish, democratic, advanced, enlightened state here.

As in our parasha, an awareness of the miraculous has been replaced by criticism, cynicism and especially complaints. So many complaints! It appears that this is not just the topic of this week's parasha. It is the timeless story of the human soul.

In Exodus Chapter 16, verses 2-3, immediately following the crossing and Song of the Red Sea, it says *"And the whole congregation of the children of Israel murmured against Moshe and against Aharon in the wilderness; and the children of Israel said to them: 'Would that we had died by the hand of the LORD in the land of Egypt, when we sat by the fleshpots, when we did eat bread to the full; for you have brought us forth into this wilderness, to kill this whole assembly with hunger.'"*

There seems to have been a Divine plan: our neighbors got all the oil and we got the songs. But even without oil, this nation of poor slaves has created such economic wealth that our forebearers could not even have dreamed of. Where did it come from? Where does any abundance come from?

"Then said the LORD unto Moshe: 'Behold, I will cause to rain bread from heaven for you; and the people shall go out and gather a day's portion every day, that I may try them, whether they will walk in My law, or not. " (16:4)

It appears that abundance comes from the sky, doesn't it? The described abundance comes with a curious addendum: *"that I may try them..."* In other words, I will put them to the test. Economic abundance is a blessing, but it is also the biggest test of all, *"whether they will walk in My law, or not."*

One kind of abundance is called "the fleshpots" and another is called "bread from heaven". What is the difference between them? It is only a matter of awareness, not quantity or gastronomy. The meat and bread are primarily in our heads or hearts. The difference between the abundance of a slave or of a free person is separated by a sea. On one side of the sea there are pots of meat, onions, garlic, squash, and other foods. On the other side there is bread from heaven, milk, and honey. What connects the two is longing. The free person longs for the unforgettable taste of the meat, and the slave longs for the mysterious bread of abundance that falls from the sky, and for the milk and honey that tastes like Eden.

"And when the layer of dew was gone up, behold upon the face of the wilderness a fine, scale-like thing, fine as the hoar-frost on the ground. And when the children of Israel saw it, they said one to another: 'What is it?'--for they knew not what it was. And Moshe said to them: 'It is the bread which the LORD has given you to eat. This is the thing which the LORD has commanded: Gather you of it every man according to his eating; an omer a head, according to the number of your persons, shall you take it, every man for them that are in his tent.' And the children of Israel did so, and gathered some more, some less. And when they did mete it with an omer, **he that gathered much had nothing over, and he that gathered little had no lack; they gathered every man according to his eating. And Moshe said to them: 'Let no man leave of it till the morning.'** *"*(16:14-18)

The wondrous manna of the desert is one of the major players in the amazing story of the journey of the People of Israel. It is, therefore, also a major player in the lives of every one of us. The manna tells us that we each always have enough, maybe even too much, and we need to take care not to hoard. Only on Friday do we need to collect for an additional day – for the Sabbath. The manna gives Shabbat its special meaning: a day on which we are absolutely sure that we have everything we need, that our lives are complete as they are.

This week, as we begin our journey in the desert, we are encouraged to consider both kinds of abundance: both kinds propel us forward, both cause us grief, and both also bring comfort. We contain both and we should familiarize ourselves with the sensation of each, for they are different. At times we are crazed by a feeling of permanent lack that is never fulfilled, that whispers to us that there is no such thing as enough. Other times we feel that *"he that gathered little had no lack; they gathered every man according to his eating."* In other words, we all have just what we need. Most of us go to the refrigerator to satisfy spiritual hunger. But most of us also know what the pleasure of heaven-sent abundance feels like. The Western world has more material abundance than it has ever had, but it is also more starved of meaning than ever.

"Behold, the days come, said the Lord GOD, that I will send a famine in the land, not a famine of bread, nor a thirst for water, but of hearing the words of the LORD." (Amos 8:11)

Are you familiar with this hunger, this thirst?

70 years have passed since the great miracle. Great hunger is felt in the Land, but do we know what we hunger for? Do we know the difference between the fleshpots and the manna?

It is time to look around, to open our eyes and to begin to collect some of the abundant manna that surrounds us endlessly, that is heaped upon us each day in this Land of Milk and Honey. How fortunate we are!

Parashat Yitro: Torah Pouring Forth Like Water

50 days have passed since that thrilling night on which we left our homes, all of our possessions, and everything that was familiar for 210 years, and set out on the most famous journey in Western history. And this week, on the 47th day following our exodus from Egypt, we can already see Mount Sinai in the distance. After three days of intensive preparation, suspense, and purifying, we are ready! And then the Mountain fills with smoke. Some of us flee in great panic as all around us we hear the sound of shofars …: *"And God spoke all these words, saying: I am the LORD your God, who brought you out of the land of Egypt, out of the house of bondage. You shall have no other gods before Me."* (Sh'mot 20:1-2)

We were all there – all of us! Not one Jew was absent as the God of Freedom listed the Ten Commandments and Thirteen Attributes (the Divine Attributes with which, according to Judaism, God governs the world). We were there, but most of us don't remember. What a shame! Since that time we have been debating two great questions:

1. Was that decisive event a one-time revelation – did it happen and then come to an end, or was it (albeit a very impressive) first instance of a series of ongoing revelations?

2. The description of the revelation is very dramatic, but it is not precise. What actually happened there? What exactly did the People of Israel hear? Our Sages tell us that all of us were there and yet heard it differently, each according to his or her spiritual development and the shape of his or her soul. Who, then, heard the version that we have before us today? Are there others?

There are two main approaches to this momentous event: The classic, traditional one which states that it was indeed a one-time event that has not repeated itself since the 6th of Sivan, the third month after leaving Egypt, on the 50th day of the journey at Mount Horev. According to this view, the further we are from the date of this event, the less we remember, and it is therefore becoming more blurred and less precise. As this happens, our spiritual level decreases and wanes, quite dwarfed by the spiritual giants who preceded us and passed its memory down through the generations: Moshe passed the Torah to Joshua, who passed it to the Elders, who passed it to the Prophets, who passed it to the members of the Sanhedrin, who passed it to our Sages, who passed it to the early commentators, who passed it to the later commentators.

In other words, the traditional, classic perception is one of dilution, of a weakening of understanding as we move further from the source. In this version, we, who represent the present, are always the most recent and therefore the weakest link in the chain.

The later, non-orthodox understanding is the reverse: we become more knowledgeable as time goes by because we know more, we have discovered more, and therefore we have a better understanding of the secrets of Creation, which continue to be revealed to us. In biblical times, for example, there were no microscopes which allowed us to see inside living structures. What could Moshe's generation understand about these? They didn't have a telescope either. They could not use one to gaze up to the heavens and understand what lies beyond the vision of the naked eye. They could not know that the Earth apparently is not the center of the universe, and that it is round, not flat. The modern approach sanctifies the new and vilifies the old. In academia, the newer the source the more reliable it is perceived to be. Moshe, according to this view, was very progressive for his time, but very primitive relative to our enlightened, Western reality.

So which is it - a one-time event or an ongoing one? The answer lies, as many important Biblical ones do, in a quiet, dark corner of the previous Torah portion, Beshalach: After the Red Sea splits in two and the Children of Israel pass through to the arid side of life, they discover they may have made a mistake, because there is no water in the desert. Without water there is no life. Surely slavery in Egypt would be preferable?

This is not a trivial question – many of us wonder about this issue practically daily: do we prefer a difficult, oppressive situation which is secure, to a life of freedom in which we are constantly aware of danger?

As there is no water, the People rant and rave. And then it happens: God commands Moshe to strike the rock, and life-giving water pours forth. But notice the description, because it contains an important detail which is usually overlooked and is the answer to our dilemma:

"And all the congregation of the children of Israel journeyed from the wilderness of Tzin, by their stages, according to the commandment of the LORD, and encamped in Rephidim; and there was no water for the people to drink... And the LORD said to Moshe: 'Pass on before the people, and take with you of the elders of Israel; and your rod, with which you smote the river, take in your hand, and go... Behold, I will stand before you there upon the rock in Horev; and you shall smite the rock, and there shall come water out of it, that the people may drink.' And Moshe did so in the sight of the elders of Israel." (Shmot 17: 1, 5-6)

The rock (which, in its form "tzur", is one of God's names) is in Horev! Horev is Mount Sinai. This means that even before the People of Israel reached Mount Sinai, God had been revealed as a source of living water! The Jewish tradition has justifiably never specifically identified the location of Mount Sinai, leaveing open the possibility that Mount Sinai is not an actual physical location but rather a concept! Mount Sinai, according to this reading, is a place where each person experiences significant revelation. The Torah is likened to Living Water. Mount Sinai - Horev - may have actually been a spring of life-giving water. If we accept this notion - of Mount Sinai being a spring of water, then we can also entertain the idea that as long as it does not dry up, it continues to flow.

Mount Sinai appears also as Har Ha'Elohim - the Mountain of God - upon which Moshe was grazing with his flocks and encountered the Divine in the burning bush:

"Now Moshe was keeping the flock of Yitro his father-in-law, the priest of Midian; and he led the flock to the farthest end of the wilderness, and came to the mountain of God, to Horev... And Moshe said to God: 'Who am I, that I should go to Pharaoh, and that I should bring forth the children of Israel out of Egypt?' And He said: 'Certainly I will be with you; and this shall be the token unto you, that I have sent you: when you have brought forth the people out of Egypt, you shall serve God upon THIS mountain.' (Sh'mot 3:1, 11-12)

So, Mount Sinai is both the mountain of the Burning Bush, and the mountain from which Moshe drew water from a rock, and finally, it is the mountain of the Torah of Living Water.

But that is not all!

We return to Mount Horev 550 years later, in one of the darkest moments of Eliyahu (Elijah) the Prophet, following the great drama on the Carmel. He escapes in great haste and is in such despair that he literally crawls with his last ounce of energy to Mount Horev, in order to drink from that same spring, in order to revive his spirit and find the answers to the quandary of his life.

As we connect the dots - the Burning Bush, the water flowing out of the rock, revelation and the giving of the Torah, and finally, Eliyahu's encounter with God at Horev - the picture that is emerging is that the spring of Living Waters at Mount Sinai flows perpetually, eternally, and should it stop, the world would dry up.

This is why, when Halacha is determined, it is never based on the Torah, but rather on "Halacha to Moshe at Sinai," in other words, we go back to that source of Living Water each time anew. A People who desires life, an individual who desires life, cannot make do with a one-time revelation of great wisdom, leaving us only with a fading, murky memory of the Divine. Each person must quench his or her thirst and be renewed by drinking from the same spring of living water.

How can we know that we are at the right place and that the water is, in fact, life-giving? If it is the place where God speaks to all beings, and yet each hears his or her own celestial melody that is written especially for them, then it is Mount Sinai/Horev.

Parashat Mishpatim: Whose Life is This, Anyway?

This week's parasha opens with the words: *"Now these are the ordinances which you shall set before them..."* The previous verses detailed the Ten Commandments, the overall framework, and now we read the practical laws that follow the heavenly ones. There are 53 such mitzvot detailed in the parasha. They deal with human relations, possessions, physical harm, and more. All are related in one way or another to the Ten Commandments.

The parasha begins with the laws of the Jewish slave and his or her right to freedom, derived from the first Commandment, *"I am the Lord your God who brings you out of the Land of Egypt, from the house of bondage."* (Sh'mot 20:2) Such a revolutionary idea! 3500 years before the American Constitution and the arrival of the Statue of Liberty in New York, the code of Jewish law opens with the divine principle of freedom. It is as though the Torah is trying to tell us that freedom is the point, and everything else is commentary; an attempt to establish this truth in our lives. This is indicated also in the shift in God's title. Previously called "the God of Avraham, Yitzchak and Yaakov" or "El Shadai", the title from here onwards is "I am the God who takes **you** out of Egypt (Mitzrayim), who takes **you** out of the narrow places (meytzarim), who takes **you** out of the house of bondage." This is stated in the present tense, meaning now, every day!

And yet Parashat Mishpatim is not really about freedom. It actually poses a much broader question: Whose life is this? This life we call ours, is it in fact ours? To whom do we owe our very breath?

89

Western society in general and Israel in particular, is torn between three possible answers to this question. The "secular" majority will answer this question in the context of human rights, saying that every human being has or should have exclusive rights of ownership to his body, his creations, his finances and his intellectual property. Believers might take a different stand, reflected in Job's eternal statement: *"God has given, God has taken away, Blessed be His name..."* Between these two approaches, the founders of Zionism (and the Kibbutz movement in which I grew up) had a third option: "Neither position is correct. Our lives belong to society, to the community, the nation", as reflected in the quote "it is good to die for our country" (attributed to pre-state hero Yoseph Trumpeldor). A less "tribal" option is that we belong to the human family.

These last two parashot – Yitro (with the Ten Commandments) and Mishpatim (this week's parasha) suggest, first and foremost, that our lives do not belong to us. Whom do they belong to, then?

As a believing person, I am tempted to go with the obvious, i.e. that our lives are God's. That is the simplest explanation, and the text does say *"for the land is Mine; for you are strangers and settlers with Me."* (Vayikra 25:23) But actually, this is too simple. What does it mean, that our lives belong to God?? If one imagines God as a father, a benevolent or a cruel boss or an ultimate referee in the game of life, then there is no problem: there is someone or something to blame for all of our misfortunes. But if one's idea of God is less concrete, then the question remains: whose life is this, anyway?

Although I squirm in discomfort as I consider my options, I will offer my answer to this momentous question. This answer is mine only, and does not obligate anyone else. But first, think about your own answer:

If your answer gives you a warm, fuzzy, happy feeling, then it is probably the right one for you, at least for now. If it feels heavy, burdensome or confusing, you need to keep looking.

My suggestion is that life belongs to itself, to infinity, to the energy of every atom and molecule in the universe. Some would call this "God" or "Creation". Others would call it "the universe" or "nature", although these are really not the same thing. In these last parashot God is identified by the words "Anochi", meaning "me", "myself" and "the vertical".

When Avraham and Moshe hear the Voice telling them to get up, go, live, and bring blessing to the world, they answer from the heart, saying "Hineni" - "Here I am."
"Hineni" may be the human version of "Anochi". It echoes the heavenly "I", saying "I am here, I am alive, You are the Source of life, and I am life itself."

When one concludes that life belongs to itself, something huge and stifling is released. Slavery melts away. Try it and see. When my life does not belong to "me" or to some collective or other, it feels much lighter. One can then begin to live, to breathe, and even death does not feel like a threat, because life… lives!

So – "Lechayim", to Life! To Freedom!

Parashat Truma: From Possession to Dedication

It is time to change gears. In fact, we are actually making a U-turn. From this week and until the end of Exodus we will be dealing with the construction of the portable Tabernacle, the Mishkan in the desert. This change begins in this week's parasha, Truma.

On Mount Sinai, all Moshe and God discuss are the minute details of building the Mishkan, including the verse: *"And let them make Me a sanctuary, that I may dwell within them."* (Sh'mot 25:8)

The verse does not say God will dwell within **it** (the Mishkan), but within **them**. This mixing of pronouns indicates that the parasha assumes that the Mishkan and the individual person are one and the same!

At the end of Exodus the building of the sanctuary will be complete and we will read: *"... So Moshe finished the work. Then the cloud covered the tent of meeting, and the **kavod** of the LORD filled the tabernacle. And Moshe was not able to enter into the tent of meeting, because the cloud abode thereon, and the **kavod** of the LORD filled the tabernacle."* (Exodus 40: 33-35)

The Hebrew word "kavod" is usually translated as "honor". Yet, it shares a root with the word "kaved", heavy. Hence, "kavod" implies the weight of presence. So the essence of the Mishkan is in being the container for God's "weight", or in spiritual terms, "presence". It is in the Mishkan that God's presence will dwell. And there He will "meet" Moshe (in the Tent of Meeting), and guide the Children of Israel in every possible way. Yet, the sentence, *"that I may dwell within them*", leaves us wondering, where is the Divine presence to be found - in the Mishkan or within us?

A central theme of Parashat Truma is actually what a person does with his or her physical abundance. This is not a question only for the well-to-do, but a challenge for each and every one of us.

Bnei Yisrael leave Egypt "heavy with possessions." Our Sages attribute the heaviness of their load to two very problematic sources. The first source is the gold and silver that the Israelites "borrowed" from their Egyptian neighbors at God's command on the eve of their departure. (The Sages were indeed troubled by that "borrowing". They explain that it served as the payment due after years of slavery and being taken advantage of). The second, heavier source is the booty, the treasures that wash ashore after the Egyptian forces drown in the Red Sea.

Yet, although the Israelites are heavy with treasures from these two sources, they have no practical use for them in the desert. This leads us to surmise that they must have another purpose – for the Israelites and for us. Just as God's "heaviness" (Kavod) will fill the Mishkan, so too, the Israelites came out of Egypt with a great "heaviness", heavy with possessions.

On a certain level, wealth and poverty are not simply a matter of numbers, but rather a question of consciousness; not a plus or a minus in the checking account; not a full refrigerator or an empty one. This is not to belittle or make light of the pain felt by those who experience need. On the contrary! We are not discussing social justice or the division of wealth. Wealth and poverty are actually two opposite points on the scale of "having" in our lives:
Wealth = the sense of "having" more than enough
Poverty = the sense of not "having" enough

To whom do all possessions belong to? Who owns them? From whom does one borrow them? We understand "possession" to imply property or wealth which is ours, in one way or another. So much of civil law is there to codify the laws of possession. As we know, laws are needed when something is not clear, not "natural", not "organic".

Possessions don't "belong". No "thing" belongs. In fact, these shouldn't even be called possessions. They just ARE. Just as the Israelites are liberated, so too is the Egyptian wealth. It is liberated from the false sense of possession, which may be the ultimate symbol of slavery.

And lest the Israelites think that the "freed Egyptian wealth" is now theirs to possess, this week they are invited (not commanded!) to let it go, to sacrifice it, to free it. How? By dedicating it to the creation of the Mishkan; by sanctifying the gold and silver for God's kavod, or presence. It is in the Mishkan - the symbol of the generosity of the heart - that God's presence will dwell.

"Imagine no possessions. I wonder if you can..." sang John Lennon so many years ago. He was right! It is not easy at all!!!

Five Parashot are needed to get this idea across. And does it work? Absolutely not! We are still trying to learn the art of sanctifying all of life and all we have; therefore we still read and reread these parashot every year.

All things are "borrowed". Nothing can be possessed. And everything, if dedicated, can become a Mishkan for Divine presence. It is a choice of generosity of the heart!

Parashat Tetzaveh:
The Bare Truth & the Garments of Reality

Last week, in Parashat Trumah, we wondered at the detailed description of the Mishkan (Tabernacle) in the desert. This week we are mystified by the details of the priestly clothing in Parashat Tetzaveh. This week we also meet the priestly cast(e) for the very first time in the Bible. This is a very significant occasion – these priests will have a central role in Jewish spiritual life for more than a thousand years, until the destruction of the Second Temple in 70 AD. Yet rather than reading about their unique tasks or about their role as the conduits of God to the people, we read about their clothes!

"And bring you near unto you Aharon your brother, and his sons with him, from among the children of Israel, that they may minister unto Me in the priest's office, even Aharon, Nadav and Avihu, Eleazar and Itamar, Aharon's sons. And you shall make holy garments for Aharon your brother, for splendor and for beauty. And you shall speak unto all that are wise-hearted, whom I have filled with the spirit of wisdom, that they make Aharon's garments to sanctify him, that he may minister unto Me in the priest's office. And these are the garments which they shall make: a breastplate, and an ephod, and a robe, and a tunic of checker work, a mitre, and a girdle; and they shall make holy garments for Aharon your brother, and his sons, that he may minister unto Me in the priest's office." (Exodus 28:1-4)

What is the significance of this detailed description of the priestly garments? And how does it fit in with the statement made earlier in Exodus, *"and you shall be unto Me a kingdom of priests, and a holy nation"* (Exodus 19:6)? This question is made more urgent by the fact that the priests are presented as the ideal to which all of Israel should strive – to be a kingdom of priests.

What is it about these garments, and about clothing in general, that warrants almost an entire parasha?

Professor Donald Hoffman of UC Irvine, in a fascinating series of articles and in a TED talk given in March, 2015, compares the human brain to a complex operating system which enables us to conceive of and function in the world. Our operating system compacts reality into molds and makes it accessible to the human brain, according to Prof. Hoffman. The two mechanisms on which the system runs are the sense of time and the sense of space. In reality, he claims, there is no time or space. The human mind translates the mystery of reality (called the "Einsof" in Judaism) into structures within which we can function.

In Jewish terms, this operating system "kicked in" at the moment the fruit of knowledge was consumed in the Garden of Eden. Not surprisingly, this is also the occasion on which the first clothes were created. Before that time, nakedness, i.e. the bare truth, was within grasp. But with their newly-acquired "knowledge", Adam and Chava were essentially fitted with the human operating system. Space became a place in which to hide from God in shame, time became the realization of mortality.

Next week, in Parashat Ki Tisa, Moshe will ask God to show him His presence, and God will respond: a person cannot see Me and live. Adam and Chava were banished from the Garden of Eden, from the possibility of witnessing the bare truth. The ingenious operating system put in its place contains many layers which enable us to live our lives.

It is precisely these layers, these "garments", with which reality is clothed, that constitute our ingenious operating system. Not only that, but the garments are really only representations of the operating system – they are not the system itself - just as the icon on a computer desktop represents an underlying program or function, which performs a task using ever-more-hidden elements of technology. In the human operating system, the connection between the final, hidden layers of bare reality and the outermost layers of garments remains a mystery to human consciousness. Our operating system allows us to make some sense of external order and meaning, while possessing a very limited understanding of the intricate layers that lie beneath the surface.

We often confuse the garments with reality, thinking that they are the truth itself rather than elements of an operating system. Eye-witness accounts are considered viable in a court of law as truth. This is the way public order is maintained, and it is the best we have. The closest we can get to God is through the very minimal, symbolic nature of our God-given operating system.

The Mishkan and the Temple are "icons" for God's presence in our world; they are the places in which people "met" their God to thank, to beg pardon, or simply to pay taxes in support of the religious institutions. They did not, however, see the unseeable God of Pure Reality; they met the priest instead. The priest was part of the operating system which included prescribed animal and grain sacrifices and specific utterances; and the priest wore prescribed garments at different stages of the ceremonies. In Deuteronomy 16:16 it says:

"Three times in a year shall all your males appear before the LORD your God in the place which He shall choose; on the Feast of

unleavened bread, and on the Feast of weeks, and on the Feast of tabernacles; and they shall not appear before the LORD empty;"

This meeting between man and God is conducted through the filter of a very well-oiled operating system, after which the pilgrim returns home feeling he has "met" God and brought Him his offerings. The pilgrim is content with what he perceives to be God's contentment with his actions.

Covers, garments, layers of cloth – the operating system described utilizes all of these: a colorful tent, a caste of priests, sacrifices, incense, and priestly outfits. Is it at all possible to see the "bare truth" under all of these? Probably not. Not as long as we are alive and subject to what Professor Hoffman calls our "human operating system."

So what is the message here? The message is that once we are aware of the inevitable limitations of our operating system and at peace with them, we are free to be more aware of the many layers, nuances and depths through which we experience God and the bare truth. We can upgrade the system and enhance it; but always remember that it is not the Truth, only the method for our limited perception of It. So far, we have not found a better system.

Parashat Ki Tisah:
The Depth of Belief, the Strength of Will

Parashat Ki Tisah is the parasha of missed opportunity.

Moshe is still on Mount Sinai. He has been there for 39 days. Tomorrow he is due to return. The Divine tablets of the Law are already written with the finger of God. Just before the happy conclusion of the story, the People lose patience:

"And when the people saw that Moshe delayed to come down from the mount, the people gathered themselves together unto Aharon, and said unto him: 'Up, make us a god who shall go before us; for as for this Moshe, the man that brought us up out of the land of Egypt, we know not what is become of him.'" (Sh'mot 32:1)

The unfortunate developments are well-known:

"And Aharon said to them: 'Break off the golden rings, which are in the ears of your wives, of your sons, and of your daughters, and bring them to me.' And all the people broke off the golden rings which were in their ears, and brought them to Aharon. And he received it at their hand, and fashioned it with a graving tool, and made it a molten calf; and they said: 'This is your god, O Israel, which brought you up out of the land of Egypt.' And when Aharon saw this, he built an altar before it; and Aharon made proclamation, and said: 'Tomorrow shall be a feast to the LORD.' And they rose up early on the morrow, and offered burnt-offerings, and brought peace-offerings; and the people sat down to eat and to drink, and rose up to make merry." (Exodus 32: 2-6)

The People couldn't wait one more day! A little more patience and the whole story would have turned out differently. There would have been no golden calf, and they (and we) might have received the miraculous, Divine tablets.

Instead, the tablets were thrown down by a furious Moshe, and we are left with the second set, the heavy, limited stone tablets written with the blunt hand of human flesh and blood when Moshe again ascended the Mountain. We will never know what was written on the first set or what God's handwriting looks like.

This missed opportunity is more than just a case of unfulfilled curiosity. Humankind has always wondered what God wants of us, anticipating that if we knew the answer to this question, the quality of our lives would be significantly different. If we knew the reason for suffering; if we knew the point of our hard work; if we knew that our lives had meaning; that they are not for naught…

But we will never know, and all because of a few hours of impatience.
How many times have we given up a moment before the end…?

It appears that in those crucial, last moments of patience and anticipation, a moment before redemption, another, cruel mechanism comes into play, and it destroys everything we have done to arrive at this critical point in time.

This is the moment in which two great forces are pitted against one another: that of belief, and that of despair. Despair convinces us that nothing good can come from waiting patiently. Belief, however, is the force that persists against all odds.

In Rabbi Nachman's famous story "The Tale of the Lost Princess", the theme of giving up a moment before redemption is powerfully presented. The princess has been taken by the "not good", and the king's assistant has gone on a journey to retrieve her. After many years, he finds her in a beautiful castle, surrounded by wonderful food and music. This is the palace of the "not good"! The princess whispers to the assistant that there is a small window of opportunity to save her, and that he must wait for her at a particular time and place, and be sure not to eat or drink on the appointed day. The assistant has every intention of fulfilling her instructions, but at the very last minute he sees a tree with very tempting fruit which he eats. He then falls into a deep slumber. The princess' carriage passes by while he is sleeping, and he wakes to find a tear-stained note from the disappointed princess. This sequence of events repeats itself time after time. The assistant continues to miss the opportunity to release the princess from the "not good" and to bring good into the world.

Sometimes it seems that the entire world is captive of the "not good", which has long ago "kidnapped" the human agenda and has been torturing it cruelly ever since. We wring our hands sadly, bemoan the "not good" in which we live, but – and this may sound unbelievable – we appear to give up a moment before the happy end because something in us recoils from redemption.

Something within us doesn't really want the "good" to come about!

I can already hear the reactions… "What is he talking about? Of course we want what is good for us! We aren't masochists!" But the truth is maybe we are… a little bit.

Clearly we all would like to be happier. But if we really, truly wanted this, we would not give up so easily. We think we want things to be better, but apparently not too much better. Because if they were, what would happen?

Who would we be without our problems?

Who would we be without the stories we tell ourselves and others about how we have been deprived in one way or another?

If we are not victims of the "not good", would we be able to meet our own expectations of ourselves?

We would have no excuses to fall back on, and this is a scary thought!

What is it about the "not good" that seduces us to spend time with it and not let go?

The "not good" creates an identity – without our pain who would we be?

The "not good" releases us from responsibility- it is not our fault that...

The "not good" motivates us to get up in the morning, because we need to prove to ourselves and to everyone else what we are worth.

The "not good" provides plenty of drama – how can one be bored when engaged in the battle of life?

Etc...

I repeat the inevitable conclusion: at the end of the day, we are happy with this "not good"! In other words, this "not good" makes us feel pretty good, or certainly good enough.

The golden calf is an Egyptian symbol. It appears that on that fateful day of impatience, the true desire of Bnei Yisrael becomes apparent. They (we) are not in search of freedom or the Promised Land. They yearn for the gods of Egypt, that place of ultimate "not good" with which they are familiar. They miss the food, the security, the water, the abundance of work. Despair in Egypt is not so "not good" and despair is a familiar companion!

In the Talmud, Masechet Makot 10B, our Sages teach us that a person is led in the path he desires. In other words, the reality of our lives reflects our deep wishes fairly accurately. Alternately, the lack of clear aspiration also creates reality. At the end of the day, there is no vacuum in nature. If our aspirations are not guiding us, someone else's will fill the void and determine our reality.

The incident of the Golden Calf teaches us a lesson about will and about belief. Perhaps the degree of our will matches the depth of our belief. Where there is no belief there is also no will. A person cannot desire what his or her belief cannot imagine.

Therefore, despite the fact that the golden calf is considered a sin, I want to suggest that it can be seen not as an opportunity that was missed, but a clarification of will. The desire for the Divine tablets was not truly present, and that is the reason for the events that followed.

If and when we really want those Divine tablets, they will be evident.
It is a matter of desire.
No… it is a matter of belief.
Or perhaps both!

Wishing you a Shabbat of peace and good desires.

Vayakhel-Pikudei:
Listening to the Wisdom of One's Heart

Three weeks ago, in Parashat Trumah, we began reading about the Mishkan (the Tabernacle in the desert). This week, if all goes well, the work will be completed and the Cloud of Kavod (Presence) will descend and fill the Mishkan.

Up until this point, the discussion of the Mishkan takes place on Mount Sinai between God and Moshe. But this week Moshe has already come down from the Mountain. He gathers the people and relates the instructions he has received over the course of the 80 days he has spent on the cloudy summit.

Many commentators raise the obvious question: Why is it necessary to hear it all again? We, the readers, were with Moshe on Mount Sinai and we heard it all already. Could we not just read that Moshe repeated the instructions he received word for word, and that Bezalel and Ohaliav followed the instructions precisely, to Moshe's full satisfaction?
Apparently not!

This is a great lesson in the transmission of information – from the Source to the messenger and from the messenger to everyone else. Does the messenger or the transmitter always stay true to the Source? Will he or she dare change anything in the message?

Although it seems that Moshe is repeating the instructions he receives very accurately, in fact, on closer inspection, this is not so! Moshe adds a very important and interesting change. Three weeks ago we read how the building instructions specified a progression from the **innermost** sanctuary **outwards** - from the most holy to the least holy. And yet here Moshe is giving instructions in the reverse order! Why is this? If the initial instructions were important and the direction (inwards-out) significant, how can the reverse be acceptable?

Last week, in Parashat Ki Tisa, we read about a unique phenomenon: *"And Moshe turned, and went down from the Mount, with the two tablets of the testimony in his hand; tablets that were written on both their sides; on the one side and on the other were they written."* (Shmot 32:15) The Divine tablets that Moshe dashes to the ground and breaks are written on both sides! It is possible to read them from both directions. The second set of tablets, which Moshe writes himself, are written on one side only (in the regular, mortal manner). What does this mean and what is the connection to the message being transmitted from the Source to humanity?

In Hebrew the words for "focus", "direction" and "intent" are all based on the same root: k.v.n (direction) and kavana (intent). Is it possible that direction and intent are a human "obsession" and of no interest to God? The Creator's perspective is of Oneness, entirely without dimension and direction. There is no external and internal, heart and skin, house and street, body and garment. All is One. Therefore, there is also no more or less holy.

If this preoccupation of ours is beside the point for God, why is it so significant to us?

The phrase "wise of heart" appears several times in this parasha, describing both men and women. The wise of heart are those who are called upon to implement the construction of the Mishkan, to connect the parts and turn a pile of raw materials into a wondrous Tent of Meeting in which God's glory can dwell.

105

It is entirely unclear what a wise heart is, and how it is different from any other kind of wisdom. It is also unclear what the connection is between wisdom of the heart and the building of the Mishkan. There are many beautiful explanations, and I would like to suggest one.

Wisdom is usually associated with an understanding of the world around us – how things work and why. The wise one, whether scientist, historian, archaeologist, doctor, engineer, looks carefully at the world and understands, or tries to understand how it all works. The heart, on the other hand, represents the internal ("the heart of the matter").

Following this logic, the wise one looks outwards and the heart directs us inwards.

Therefore, combining the words "wisdom of the heart" implies a Divine quality, as exemplified in the first Tablets – the Divine Tablets which could be read in both directions. The "wisdom of the heart" is of a unique, Divine sort, which does not distinguish between one thing and another, between external and internal, between more and less, or even between holy and profane. Wisdom of the heart is the wisdom of unity, of Oneness!

The wise person is blessed with the ability to distinguish between right and wrong, good and evil, one thing and another, high and low, worthy and unworthy and so on.

A person who is wise of heart does not dwell on these distinctions. This wisdom is without hierarchy or judgment. Most of my readers may wonder: without judgment? How can that be good? The ability to distinguish between right and wrong, good and bad is a building block of human consciousness! That is why we call it wisdom! Perhaps we should use the word "knowledge" instead. But the wise of heart, according to the description above, see something else. They see wholeness.

The values we place on things are subjective, and the hierarchy we assign is based entirely on our education and culture. For most of us, there is no equality at all between people or things. The ability to make distinctions is an essential part of our value system, which places more weight on what we consider to be good and right. Even the word "value" implies a subjective measurement. Yet, according to Divine, eternal principles, this apparently is not the case. A grain of sand is like a mountain, a cell is like an entire body, and an animal is not different from a human being.

King Solomon said: *"For that which befalls the sons of men befalls beasts; even one thing befalls them; as the one dies, so dies the other; yea, they have all one breath; so that man has no preeminence above a beast; for all is vanity."* (Kohelet 3:19) In other words, there is no difference between man and beast – they have one spirit, and any attempt at hierarchy is vanity (or vapor = hevel).

I know this way of thinking is challenging. Here is an exercise that may help:

Stop a moment; look around – at people, furniture, objects, at your body – with open eyes. Listen well to the stirrings of your heart and mind, to the inner chatter, the endless judgments and preferences. Try to put all of this "noise" aside, and let everything just be – without judgment, without assigning value or preference. Try for a moment to know that everything is as it should be, in its place, including the anger, the frustration, the happiness, even the slight headache and the mess in the house, even the dishes in the sink, the noise from the television and the list of chores.. Everything is 100% itself, entirely whole.

107

This method of observation or meditation requires much practice, but " ... *it is not too hard for you, neither is it far off... It is not in heaven... neither is it beyond the sea... But the word is very near unto you, in your mouth, and in your heart, that you may do it."* (D'varim 30:11-14)

I practice this observation often, and suddenly a Mishkan appears and the Godly that is in all things is present, and a moment of wisdom of the heart becomes a sense of wondrous, eternal Oneness.

And then we return to our regular form of wisdom – the one that sorts and prefers, evaluates and critiques, judges, and reduces. That too, is fine. It, too, is whole and perfect just as it is.

I wish you a Shabbat full of wisdom of the heart; for it is there we can find a true Shabbat Shalom.

Parashat Vayikra: The Art of Giving

This week we begin a new book, a very unique book. It is the book called "Torat Hakohanim", the Bible of the Priests, which is actually another name for the Book of Leviticus or Vayikra.

We begin this book with great anticipation, although its first chapters do not make for easy reading. They describe the sacrifices and a wide variety of dermatological ailments in great detail. It is tempting to just give up on the entire book, but please resist! Vayikra is a very important book. It teaches us the most hidden secrets about forging relationships with ourselves, with others, and with God. It teaches us how to draw near. Its climax is the eternal verse: "You shall love your neighbor as yourself" (Vayikra 19:18). But before we get to this verse, we will have to deal with the dilemma of sacrifices.

Parashat Vayikra deals exclusively with the sacrifices that the Cohanim perform in the newly completed Tabernacle. We read about five kinds of sacrifices in this parasha, and we will read about others in the chapters to come:

Burnt Offering, which a person brings voluntarily. The offering is of beef, mutton or fowl, and is burnt entirely on the altar with nothing left for the priest to eat.
Meal Offering – an offering of thanksgiving made of meal and oil – a vegetarian sacrifice!
Peace Offering, which is eaten by the priest and by the person who brings it, after it has been sacrificed.
Sin Offering, which is brought by a person who has sinned unintentionally. This sacrifice atones for that sin.

Guilt Offering – a sacrifice which is brought out of regret for sins which are committed, or for an action which may have been a sin.

Don't worry – this will not be an instruction manual for the slaughtering and grilling of animals! We will see, instead, that we need this parasha, and perhaps a few more like it, because the task of giving (offering) to achieve closeness is not an easy one. Closeness and intimacy can be very scary. We fear that we will disappear in the process. At times we think we want closeness, we are sure we do, but actually, unconsciously, we do everything in our power to avoid it. We do our best to prevent being hurt or disappointed. We have many complex methods of keeping our distance: blaming others, finding fault with them, etc. But beneath this distancing, which is always based on fear, lays a deep desire for intimacy.

Intimacy can be achieved in many ways. Truth is the first and the most powerful. It is most effective when it is compassionate, when it seeks what is good and right. Accusations, judgment, gossip – these are often wrapped in an appearance of truth, but they are definitely not! I will go so far as to say that if the "truth" that we identify is not one of compassion but only of judgment, it is not the real thing.

Because the compassionate truth is perhaps the most difficult for us and leaves us feeling that achieving intimacy is almost impossible, Vayikra does not ask this of us. Instead, we are told very clearly that an attainable way to come closer is through giving.

In Hebrew the root of the words "sacrifice" and "closeness" is the same: ק.ר.ב. The first three Torah portions in Vayikra all deal with achieving closeness through offering sacrifices. Being willing to give is not easy, just as achieving compassionate truth is not. Our natural inclination is to do the reverse: when challenged we

110

withdraw, protect ourselves, raise our defenses, take no risks and sometimes even try to achieve higher ground. Parashat Vayikra invites us to try a very powerful method instead: whenever we feel difficulty, injury or an inability to move forward – these are the times to practice giving!

Giving releases pent-up energy. It reverses the flow from accepting to extending, and in doing so, initiates a dynamic of repair. Giving can begin in a small way (although the intent must be sincere), and then it will broaden into a bundle of flowing, life-giving energy.

This is the premise of the holiday of Purim, which we just celebrated. The shift in fortune of the Jews of Persia is marked by acts of giving – Mishloach Manot and alms for the poor.

Maimonides emphasizes how preferable giving is to our natural tendency to take and save things for ourselves: "It is better to abound in gifts to the poor than to have a large feast… because there is nothing more festive than noticing the poor, the orphaned, and the stranger. Gladdening the hearts of the downtrodden is like the Holy Presence." (Rambam, Laws of Megillah and Hanuka 2:15)

Many years have passed. The Mishkan was dismantled, the Temple destroyed. The sacrifices are no longer offered. But neither the prophets nor our Sages were concerned by this. They determined very clearly that different kinds of giving would replace the sacrificial offerings: "For I desire mercy, and not sacrifice, and the knowledge of God rather than burnt-offerings." (Hoseah 6:6)

My suggestion for this week is to notice opportunities for giving. When you're weary, feeling sad (or bad, or stressed) – give something, even something small.

Parashat Tzav: Every Breath We Take

If you survived last week's Torah portion, Vayikra, you are ready to take another step into the depths of the laws of sacrifices. This next step may seem a little less sweet, a little more daring; even radical. And some of my readers may object. All comments are welcome, as always!

The first part of Parashat Tzav repeats the list of sacrifices we read about and explained last week, this time from the point of view of the priests - the Cohanim – what they are and are not allowed to eat.

The second part of the parasha deals with the grand opening of the Mishkan, the Tabernacle. This event lasts eight days. During the first seven days the priests are officially given their job description, and on the eighth day tragedy strikes. We will read about it next week.

This parasha is called Tzav, "Command". This form of expression may sound a little harsh to the modern ear. Jewish tradition is careful to describe the relationship between God and Israel as a mutual, loving one, albeit complex and stormy at times. On the one hand, *"You shall love the Lord your God"* (D'varim 6:5, and from the prayer book), and on the other *"Our God, You have loved us with a timeless love, and with great and excessive compassion"* (also from the prayer book, just before the Sh'ma). There you have it – mutual love!

The best word to describe this relationship in a Jewish sense is a Covenant. This covenant is first mentioned in Parashat Noah. It appears in the form of a rainbow after the Flood, together with the promise God makes that He will not cause such devastation again. The covenant appears a second time in connection with Avraham. Then, on the journey of the People of Israel, this covenant takes on a formal, legal aspect. In a few weeks we will read this beautiful verse: *"And I will walk among you, and I will be your God, and you shall be My people."* (Vayikra 26:12) There appears to be deep mutuality in the relationship between the Creator and his creations.

This is a very interesting and sweet theology. But the laws of the sacrifices in the first three portions of Vayikra indicate quite to the contrary! The covenant between God and humans and between God and the People of Israel is entirely one-way!

As we said – the name of this portion, "Command", implies that we are reading about a commandment, and commandments are in essence one-way – given and received. Have you ever tried to command the Creator to do something? I know this is difficult for the modern, post-modern, liberal, secular ear. Yet it is worth continuing. If you are having trouble with the words "God" or "the Creator", just use whatever word you are comfortable with, such as "Reality", and you will see that we are all discussing precisely the same thing.

Think about your own life: in your experience (not your belief or your thoughts!) did you choose to be born? Does your life always reflect your desires and your choices? Will you get to choose whether, how, and when to leave this world?

If your honest answer is "yes", really and truly "yes", then you are extremely fortunate! I wish I could say the same. And I am not alone. Most of us experience challenges and difficulties which we feel are not of our choosing. We do not want them and would be very happy to forego them. If asked, we would definitely say we want other, easier, softer and more pleasant experiences, even if, in retrospect, we have learned and grown through our difficulties. But we had no choice in the matter.

Reality forces itself upon us, and so does God. This is not religious coercion! This is coercion by life itself. The more we desire something, the more life demands sacrifice! Every goal, every vision, comes at a cost. It is as though reality tells us over and over: Sacrifice! Sacrifice!

A very well-known and real example is the modern State of Israel. Its establishment was both a necessity and the fulfillment of a dream, a wonderful dream. We have been fortunate to live in these times of national renewal, and yet the sacrifices we have been asked to make are tremendous: The best and bravest of our children; the prime years of youth which are spent defending our country. Weary soldiers making their way home on the weekends. Parents of these soldiers worrying night after night, checking their cell phones for messages – these are sacrifices.

Another common but excellent example is parenthood. Beginning with pregnancy, when the mother's body makes way for a fetus, organs pressed to the side, skin, flesh and muscles stretched, all to bring new life into the world. Once it is here, we sacrifice nights of sleep, freedom of movement, and financial gain – all in order to continue the human race, as we are innately programmed to do.

So what does this all mean? In the Ethics of the Fathers, 4:22, there is a famous and very difficult description (part of which appears in the funeral service as well): *"Those who are born will die... Let not your heart convince you that the grave is your escape; for against your will you are formed, against your will you are born, against your will you live, against your will you die..."*

In other words – nobody really asked us. We were "thrown" into life, and life is a continuous process of sacrifice. Not because life is bad, not at all! As long as we have our own desires, hopes, dreams and visions, we must also recognize and accept that these come at a price. The only way to avoid this price is to stop having desires, hopes and dreams. How terrible that would be, and how ironic that life is not possible without desiring it: every breath we take is an expression of our desire for life. Every step we take is in answer to some need or desire. Even our desire has been forced upon us!

The book of Vayikra reminds us that there is a Maker to whom everything belongs. Some of us call it God, some of us call it Reality. Anyone who tries to get around It is joining Sisyphus as he repeatedly rolls his rock up the mountain.

If you find this discouraging, think again, because you have missed the point. A tremendous opportunity is being given to us, one which many of us will find too big to accept. It is the opportunity to embrace our sacrifices, to try to enjoy them, to see them as a right rather than an obligation. Since it is our reality, we are asked to consider how to live it as lovingly as possible. The Creator may love us, his creations, but I am not counting on it. I am, instead, planning how I can fulfill my side of the covenant, how I can love God, Reality, Life.

"And you shall love" - to sacrifice for your Creator, your life, your reality – *"with all your heart, with all of your soul and with all of your might."*

Shabbat Shalom, and may your week of sacrifice prepare you for a joyous and meaningful holiday.

Parashat Shmini: Initiation by Fire

I found it very difficult to write this drasha because the parasha is so charged. It is a parasha in which mistakes are made at great cost.

From a certain age a person learns about different kinds of fire: the fire that burns within - that which is his and that which is not, the collective flame and the personal one; the fire that brings blessing, and that which heralds disaster. We try to learn to distinguish between them and to be careful, because we know one does not play with fire.

Nadav and Avihu, two of Aharon's sons, play with fire and are not only burned, but are burned to death. This happens on the day of the inauguration of the Mishkan, witnessed by all of Bnei Yisrael, as the first priestly family presides over the ceremony.

This event is so dramatic that it shifts the entire focus of the parasha away from the priests and the Mishkan, to the topic of fire. Fire is the most vital element of the Mishkan. In the previous parasha we read *"Fire shall be kept burning upon the altar continually; it shall not go out."* (Vayikra 6:6)

Fire is the sign of life, of vitality. As long a person has a fire burning within him or her, he is alive, kicking, warm, moving, and functioning in the world.

Fire appears in two different places in this parasha, each dramatic and extremely significant:

"And Aharon lifted up his hands toward the people, and blessed them; and he came down from offering the sin-offering, and the burnt-offering, and the peace-offerings. And Moshe and Aharon went into the tent of meeting, and came out, and blessed the people; and the glory of the LORD appeared unto all the people. And there came forth fire from before the LORD, and consumed upon the altar the burnt-offering and the fat; and when all the people saw it, they shouted, and fell on their faces." (Vayikra 9:22-24)

At the beginning of the parasha the fire is not yet burning in the Mishkan. Only when Aharon comes and blesses the People on his own, and then again, with Moshe, does the Eternal fire come down and kindle the first flames of the altar. The People are amazed and moved. Fire appears again immediately following this event:
"And Nadav and Avihu, the sons of Aharon, took each of them his censer, and put fire therein, and laid incense thereon, and offered strange fire before the LORD, which He had not commanded them. And there came forth fire from before the LORD, and devoured them, and they died before the LORD." (Vayikra 10:1-2)

In the middle of the ceremony, Nadav and Avihu, Aharon's sons, approach. They do not bear blessings, but only the personal pans for burning incense. The previous fire had descended from above, whereas this fire is being brought by these priests as individuals on their own incense burners.

Suddenly, a Divine fire appears from the altar, a jealous, burning flame which kills them.

This event is very confusing, and its significance has been the source of many interpretations, ranging from blaming the two sons for an overabundance of pride, to the opposite argument, whereby they are consumed by the flames of religious zealotry out of love of God.

117

The two sons of Aharon and lovers such as those described in Shir Hashirim (the Song of Songs): *"Who is this that comes up from the wilderness, leaning upon her beloved? Under the apple-tree I awakened you...for love is strong as death, jealousy is cruel as the grave; the flashes thereof are flashes of fire, a very flame of the LORD. Many waters cannot quench love, neither can the floods drown it;"* (8:5-7)

Parashat Shmini is not only the parasha of the inauguration of the Mishkan, but also, and perhaps mostly, a parasha initiating the priests, thereby giving guidelines for all of us. Initiation is a process by which a person becomes acquainted with fire – its power, its qualities, jealousies, subtleties, and strengths. The subtleties of fire are the subtleties of life, and every situation requires a different kind of fire. The quality of our life matches the quality of the fire which animates us.

The difference between education and initiation (which have the same root ח.נ.כ) in Hebrew) is that the former trains or shapes, whereas the latter deals with the art of life and animation, and the distinction between different kinds of fire (male, female, parental, human, divine). As we become acculturated and socialized we lose touch with our natural instincts. The complex behavior of human beings is the source of many blessings, but these may be at the cost of our natural powers and energies. Polite, politically correct society dictates norms which, while important, bear the price of liveliness, of spontaneity and vitality.

This relationship with fire has developed over time. Cavemen knew how to bring existing fire into their caves, preserving it so that it did not go out. Their descendants learned how to use flint to make fire. Matches, cigarette lighters – all of these were logical, technical developments. Aharon, on the other hand, knew how to summon Divine fire through blessing! This is an art that is known by few!

In the general, public debate over the future of the Jewish people, there is discussion about the possibility of renewed sacrifices in the Third Temple; there is an ongoing search for the perfect red heifer; there are statements about how and when the Messiah may arrive. But the most significant question to be asked is – who will teach us Aharon's blessing? Who will initiate us into the ability to seek peace and love among people as Aharon did? These are what will rekindle the Divine fire with us.

Parashat Tazria-Metzora: We Can Breathe!

As Passover comes to an end and Shabbat begins, we arrive at the combined parasha that we all try to avoid – Tazria-Metzora. But, as you know, there is no such thing as a bad parasha. In fact, each one is *the* most amazing parasha there is. Truly!

The art of interpreting biblical text is in finding the essence of life and the meaning of the universe in each and every parasha. With this in mind, the text of Vayikra, may be approached with utmost anticipation.

The beginning of this parasha seems very problematic:
"Speak unto the children of Israel, saying: If a woman be delivered, and bear a man-child, then she shall be unclean seven days; ...And she shall continue in the blood of purification three and thirty days; But if she bear a maid-child, then she shall be unclean two weeks, as in her impurity; and she shall continue in the blood of purification threescore (60) and six days."(Vayikra 12:2-5)

Seven days of impurity for a male offspring, two weeks for a female. 33 days of purification after the birth of a male, and 66 days after a female! This formula is distressing, and raises many questions, such as:

- What is impurity?
- Why is a woman impure after giving birth – is there something essentially wrong with the process?
- And the most difficult question is why is there a distinction made between the birth of a male and a female?

The text immediately adds another difficulty:

"And when the days of her purification are fulfilled, for a son, or for a daughter, she shall bring a lamb of the first year for a burnt-offering, and a young pigeon, or a turtle-dove, for a sin-offering, to the door of the tent of meeting, to the priest. And he shall offer it before the LORD, and make atonement for her; and she shall be cleansed from the fountain of her blood. This is the law for her that bears, whether a male or a female." (Vayikra 12:6-7)

Let us first try to understand the concepts of purity and impurity, putting aside the values we tend attribute to each. Impurity is not "bad" in the normal sense of the word, nor is it a kind of dirt. The truth is we do not really know what impurity is or was. The word seems to come from a different dimension, from a completely different way of viewing reality.

We can infer from the laws that the ultimate form of impurity is death. Seen in this light, we can say that death = impurity, and life = purity. From this distinction, we may derive relative states of purity as well: something that contains a measure of death also contains a degree of impurity.

There are two biblical laws pertaining to impurity that remain to this day. The best- known is the impurity of a woman during her menstrual cycle. An egg which had the potential for life (i.e. purity) was not fertilized, thereby causing the loss of this potential - i.e. impurity. (In biblical times the loss of sperm was included in this equation, and therefore any emission that lacked the potential to take seed was considered impure. Over time and for a variety of reasons, the laws pertaining to sperm became less stringent.)

The second surviving law of impurity is the ban on the entrance of a Cohen to a cemetery, other than for the burial of an immediate family member. The Cohen, as the priest, symbolized purity, and therefore the law sought to minimize his contact with human death. Animal death, in the form of sacrifices which were the Cohanim's "bread and butter", did not fit into this equation, and is a topic for another time.

In this way, Parashat Tazria-Metzora teaches us an interesting lesson about the holiness of life. Not the holiness that we interpret as saving or extending life at any cost; not the fear of death and the denial of its imminence; but rather a great celebration of the life-force that flows in all things which are alive; the energy that flows through and around us and maintains all of Creation at all times.

The question remains – why is a distinction made between the birth of a boy and that of a girl? Please read the following explanation with an open mind – it may sound very foreign by contemporary cultural standards.

A woman has an amazing ability to bring new life into the world. This ability is almost God-like! The only problem is that all living things must die, and the more life there is, the more death there will be. This is almost a mathematical equation, but in reality it also reflects the distinction being discussed: When a boy is born there is great joy, but also much trepidation as we seek to protect this new life from harm. When a girl is born the joy is even greater, as she brings with her the potential for additional, future life. Yet this potential also heightens the expectation of additional termination of life. This is one reason for doubling the period of impurity of a mother following the birth of a girl.

But why a sin-offering?? And why is it the same following the birth of a girl or a boy? There are a few possible answers. Some are simple and superficial. Others are very deep. One simplistic answer is that during birth, when experiencing extreme pain, a woman may curse God, her husband, or even the child being born, and wish she did not have the ability to give birth. She brings a sin-offering as a way of clearing the air of those curses, regardless of whether the baby is male or female.

A different, deeper explanation follows, but once again, be prepared to open your modern ear and restrain knee-jerk objections.

From the moment of our birth and especially as our self-consciousness develops, we are in a kind of continuous competition with God. From our point of view, our life takes precedence over everything else. Clearly (we think), our survival is the most important thing in the world. A person will do absolutely anything in order to guarantee survival. Animals, too, will use their natural instincts for self-preservation, but as far as we know, they do not attribute supreme value to it. Again, as far as we know, the "personal" level in the animal kingdom is of much less importance. When the animal's time comes to return its spirit to the Creator and its body to the ground, it will do so with much greater ease than his fellow creatures - us humans - tend to do. We hold onto life with all our might, mourn it greatly when it ends, and often remain bitter, angry or accusing when our loved ones are "taken" from us.

I would like to suggest that in a sense, this is the original sin. Don't worry; I do not want to cast doubt on our desire for life or to criticize our grasping it as we do. These are natural, and appear to have an important evolutionary role. But such feelings do contain a degree of primordial accusation directed towards God. Let us recall the definition of wickedness which brought on the mythic flood in the time of Noah: *"And the LORD saw that the wickedness of man was great in the earth, and that every imagination of the thoughts of his heart was only evil continually."* (Bereishit 6:5)

From God's response to this wickedness several verses earlier, we may deduce the sin. There we read: *" And the LORD said: 'My spirit shall not abide in man forever, for that he also* [like the animals] *is flesh; therefore shall his days be a hundred and twenty years.'"* (6:3) The sin appears to be the human desire to outwit God's intentions and to live forever. (In Hebrew the words for "outwit" and "forever" share the same root: נ.צ.ח.)

Where does all of this lead us? There are many possible conclusions, the first and foremost of which is a favorite topic of mine: this is a call for humility. After the birth of a baby we tend to boast about the new life we brought into the world, but this isn't accurate. We are simply vehicles for new life. Any attempt to take credit for our lives, our existence, our successes, and eventual waning is a basic misconception.

This suggested attitude can be very liberating! We are not responsible! As the name Jew (Yehudi) implies, our task is to give thanks and credit (also from the same root) to our Creator who gives us life each and every moment. Thank God - we can breathe!

I end with the beloved verse *"Who is the man that desires **life**, and loves days, that he may see **good** therein?"* (Tehillim 34:13) Because life = purity = good. Not in the narrow, judgmental, utilitarian sense, but in the broad meaning of loving all of life, not just that which flows in the limited organism called "me". To life!

Parashat Achrei Mot-K'doshim: Radical Intimacy

We have two Torah portions this week (on a non-leap year these two short portions are combined, because there are more portions than weeks in the year).

The first of the two, Achrei Mot, is familiar to us from the Yom Kippur service. We read the first part on the morning of the holiday and the second part in the afternoon.

The second Torah portion, K'doshim, is full of instructions for a fulfilling life, including the wonderful, groundbreaking "Love your neighbor as yourself."

Achrei Mot opens with the verse *"And God spoke to Moshe after the death of the two sons of Aharon when they came close to God and died."* (Leviticus 16:1) Remember the disaster that befell Aharon two weeks ago? Last week we heard nothing about it, and this week we are reminded of Nadav and Avihu who sacrificed a "strange fire" in the Tabernacle on the day it was dedicated. As a result of this deed, a fire came out of the altar and burned them to death! That disaster left us all somewhat confused, but this week the dense cloud of uncertainty clears somewhat. God instructs us how to behave when coming close to the core, to holiness. In a similar theme, we learn about the role of the Cohen Gadol in the Temple on Yom Kippur. We read about his preparations for the most intimate of meetings in the most intimate of places on the most intimate of days. And then, on a similar theme, we are instructed with whom we may have sexual relations.

As you can see – Parashat "Achrei Mot" is all about intimacy.

Parashat K'doshim, which follows, deepens the journey into the world of intimacy even further. It begins with the verse *"And God spoke to Moshe saying: speak to all of the congregation of Israel. Tell them 'you shall be holy because I, the Lord your God am holy.'"* (Leviticus 19:2) Three times in this parasha these words are repeated. The climax is the sentence which Rabbi Akiva called the great rule of the Torah: *"And you shall love your neighbor as yourself."* (19:18)

In the verses quoted below there are several types of encounters between people: tzeddakah, morality, fairness, decency, judgmentภ and how to treat those who are weak. These encounters are the main theme of K'doshim, and one may argue, that it is precisely due to these human encounters, that K'doshim may be considered the core of the entire Torah. The famous Jewish philosopher Martin Buber would call these encounters I-You relationships. What turns a human encounter into an I-You relationship is the presence of a third entity. That third entity makes itself known repeatedly, like a bookend between every type of human encounter. Although the identity of that third party is obvious, for the purposes of clarity I highlighted its appearance:

" 'When you reap the harvest of your land, do not reap to the very edges of your field or gather the gleanings of your harvest. Do not go over your vineyard a second time or pick up the grapes that have fallen. Leave them for the poor and the foreigner. **I am the LORD your God.** *Do not steal. Do not lie. Do not deceive one another. Do not swear falsely by My name and so profane the name of your God.* **I am the LORD.** *Do not defraud or rob your neighbor. Do not hold back the wages of a hired worker overnight. Do not curse the deaf or put a stumbling block in front of the blind, but fear your God.* **I am the LORD.** *'Do not pervert justice; do not show partiality to the poor or favoritism to the great, but judge your neighbor fairly. Do not go about spreading slander among your*

126

*people. Do not do anything that endangers your neighbor's life. **I am the LORD**. Do not hate a fellow Israelite in your heart. Rebuke your neighbor frankly so you will not share his guilt. Do not seek revenge or bear a grudge against anyone among your people, but love your neighbor as yourself, **I am the LORD**.... Stand up in the presence of the aged, show respect for the elderly and revere your God, **I am the LORD**. When a foreigner resides among you in your land, do not mistreat them. The foreigner residing among you must be treated as your native-born. Love them as yourself, for you were foreigners in Egypt, **I am the LORD your God.** Do not use dishonest standards when measuring length, weight or quantity. Use honest scales and honest weights, an honest ephah and an honest hin, **I am the LORD your God, who brought you out of Egypt."** *(Leviticus 19)*

Parashat K'doshim is very clear in teaching us that relationships become intimate due the third entity's presence. However, it would not be too much of a leap to suggest that the experience of intimacy IS the experience of God's presence. Furthermore, intimacy may actually BE the essence of God.

This all sounds lovely… lofty… and perhaps not new. Yet, most would ask at this point, "How is that third entity brought in?" I would argue that before we ask about God's presence, we should ask who are the other two entities involved? If one of them is "I", who is the second? With whom we are called to be intimate? In other words, who is the "neighbor" that I am commanded to love as myself?

"Your neighbor" is actually a poor translation. The word in Hebrew is "re'acha". This word alone justifies studying Hebrew seriously! Furthermore, even the confusing prefix, "le", before "re'acha", demands our full attention. "Love your neighbor" is a totally incorrect translation! "Le" means unto and "re'acha" could just as easily have been translated as "your peer" or "your friend", but it is so much broader than that.

More than anything, "re'acha" is the ultimate "other", everything that is not I.

There is a very familiar notion that each person is a living and breathing individual, and as such, is special and unique, created in God's image. Modern Western thought has fallen in love with this idea, whereby the more one loves oneself, the more one is able to love the other, and vice-a-versa: a person who hates himself will hate the other as well.

Yet, the Bible does not say that, and I would like to question the whole premise of individuality. A person is not necessarily an individual at all, nor is he or she special or unique. Furthermore, there are no "neighbors".

The story of Creation tells us that in the beginning God "created." The Hebrew word is for created is "bara". "Bara", or "created, originally meant "externalized" ("bar" means "outside"). Following this explanation, God's creation is the externalization of Himself! This is not too far-fetched, but it does have deep ramifications: God, the One, is the source of all creation. The only "individual" in this entire saga called "Creation", is God. All else is an externalization of that One God.

"I am God", the Torah tells us; there is nothing else. And because humans are created in God's image, we, too, externalize. One's neighbor or the "other" is actually a projection of oneself onto another. There isn't really an "other", only endless projections of oneself.

This is why "Love your neighbor as yourself" could mean that your neighbor or "the other" is an exact projection of yourself. The Hebrew language loves this idea: "le re'acha" translates also into "your very own evil side"! It is our inner evil that we have difficulty containing. How fitting it is that we project it onto others!

How perfectly fitting it is, that the mechanism mentioned in Parashat "Acharei Mot" for getting rid of Israel's collective transgressions, is that of the "Se'ir Le'azazel" – the ceremony of projecting all of Israel's sins onto a scapegoat, which is then cast away, and sent off of a cliff.

How would the world look if we lived our lives with this understanding, i.e., that the "other" is actually ourselves projected? True, the "other" appears so different from us, but that is only because we cannot fully contain those parts within ourselves that are shameful in our eyes. We much prefer seeing them outside of ourselves.

What would our world look like if we knew with great clarity that all there is is "God" externalized in infinite ways? Hence all projections of the Divine are Divine too; our own limited reality is God's projection "twice removed" – God projects us, and we, in God's perfect image – the good and the (so called) "bad" - project ourselves externally, and create… our neighbor, i.e., the ultimate other!

Would we take more responsibility? Would we be more loving? Parashat "Achrei Mot" and "K'doshim" are the Hebrew version of "Radical Intimacy".

Parashat Emor: Before We Rush to Change Things

This week's parasha, Emor, deals exclusively with the holiness of the Cohanim. It focuses on two main topics: The first is the restrictions and limitations placed on the Cohanim, particularly on the Cohen Gadol, the High Priest. These include whom he is allowed to marry and which funerals he may attend. Restrictions also apply to physical imperfections which prohibit a Cohen from performing his duties. The second topic is the Jewish calendar, and the sacrifices the Cohanim were to bring on each festival.

There were very definite castes within the Israelite People, and they were not based on ability or talent, but on genealogy.

The highest and most exclusive caste was that of the Cohanim. Only the male offspring of Aharon were admitted into this group, and none were allowed to leave. If a Cohen breached the rules set out in this parasha by marrying against the prescribed rules, he became a "halal", meaning "without the holiness of the priesthood" and without the honors and responsibilities of a Cohen. He remained part of the caste, and could return to his duties should he divorce. Aharon is from the tribe of Levi, therefore all Cohanim are Levites (but not all Levites are Cohanim.)

The next caste is that of the educators, the supporters of the priesthood and the bearers of the tools of the Mishkan. These are the members of the tribe of Levi who are not the offspring of Aharon. This, too, is a closed caste which one must be born into and may not leave.

The third caste is called Israel. It is a fairly large club whose members include everyone who is an Israelite but not a Cohen or

Levy. The Cohen and Levite caste membership is transferred by paternity, whereas the Israelite caste membership is transmitted maternally. This caste may be joined, but not left! One can relinquish one's Israeli passport, but not one's Jewish heritage.

This caste system is very foreign to modern ideas of equality. It perpetuates a closed, rigid system in which one is limited by birth, gender and parentage.

The Women of the Wall have been waging a campaign to allow daughters of Cohanim to say Birkat Cohanim (the Priestly Blessing) at the Kotel. This issue came up in our Kehillah several years ago as well, and caused much strife and division.

This caste system is so foreign to us today that we preserve it only as a symbolic reminder of the Temple. Therefore, it is very difficult for me to identify with the struggle of the b'not Cohen for equality within the priesthood. How can there be equality within a system which perpetuates class distinctions and limitations posed by physical imperfections?

I am not equating this struggle with that of gender equality in general. For instance, the title "Rav" is not dependent on genealogy, but on knowledge and qualification. There is no reason a woman cannot be a rabbi. This is not the case for priesthood.

Perhaps the destruction of the Temple was God's way of bringing the caste system to an end. Our Sages left a few remnants of caste honor for the Cohanim, like the right to have the first aliya to the Torah. They even absolved us of dealing with the question of what the social order will be if and when the Third Temple is built. Their answer is that this discussion can wait for the coming of the Messiah, when everything will be different in any case.

As a male, I have learned to be very careful about issues of gender equality. The very just struggle for equality is not just intellectual, logical, or theoretical. It has very deep roots in the experience of weakness, helplessness, and dispossession. A person who has not experienced such hardship cannot truly understand this pain of discrimination. A person who has not experienced the hand of the strong and ruthless cannot truly understand the fear, paralysis, and terror that may be the consequence.

However, just as it is important to beware of gender pitfalls, we should also beware of deriding truths that were considered holy to past generations. As a traditional person I have tremendous respect for the accumulated wisdom of our Forefathers and Mothers. This wisdom is the reason I am a traditional Jew. I recognize that my predecessors saw things that I am unable to see at the moment, either because of my cultural conditioning or because of my limitations as a person. At the end of the day, just as only the tip of an iceberg is visible, so it is with most things. Ninety percent is submerged and only ten percent may be observed. The older I get, the more I am convinced that this is true of the human brain as well.

What, then, is an eternal truth that can we glean from this week's parasha? Here is one small but very significant one: humility!

The challenges that the parasha presents us with - the castes, the prohibitions due to imperfections, and the sacrifices on festivals – all of these raise the question: what is right for me? What can I ask for, and should there be a limit to my aspirations?

I often write about identifying one's aspirations and fulfilling them. This week I would like to elaborate on what appears to be the opposite position. Humility requires us to accept reality as it is. Here is part of my reality:

I was born in Israel, on a kibbutz in the Galilee, to two Jewish parents, making me a Jew by birth. I am male, white, and blue-eyed like my mother. In every other way I am like my father. My hair is graying, I wear reading glasses, I am 54 years old and my body is not getting younger.

These are all facts. Some, like my hair color and other signs of age, can be hidden. But why? Why would I/we want to change?

There seem to be many reasons to change. There are those who say that Israel is not a good place to raise children; that the neighborhood is not the best; that peace and quiet are an illusion; that we are sitting on the mouth of a volcano and living in denial. Just a week after Yom Hashoah there is no need to elaborate on the dangers of belonging to the Jewish people.

It isn't possible to change the past, but it is certainly possibly to effect the present and the future. But this is my point: What would our lives look like if we considered accepting reality as it is – totally – without wishing to change it?

Being a Jew, I will answer my question with another one: Why should I? Why should I accept that which is unpleasant, uninteresting, not gratifying? Why accept reality as is, if it is possible to improve upon it?

I am all for change when it is possible and desirable. But accepting things as they are is much harder, it appears. I find it amazing how quickly we look to improve what we find fault with. We are less able to see the vast majority of what is good, and seek, instead, to "fix" what isn't. I am not suggesting that this is wrong, just that we be able to pause and notice the difference between our automatic impulse to change and improve, and what is actually, truly in need of change. What would our lives look like if we spent time consciously accepting our situation as it is, at least for now?

What feelings do this conscious acceptance and pausing trigger? Acceptance may, indeed, bring to the surface all of our resistance to the current situation. Frustration, anger, sadness - all of these feelings are acceptable too, because they are part of reality, though they are difficult to contain, and we do everything in our power to make them go away.

But what if we do not shy away from these feelings? What if we accept them as part of reality, even for a few moments? What may happen is that the urgent need to bring change may not feel so acute. Perhaps the situation may seem much better than we previously thought. Even if it isn't, it may become clearer because we made time and space to observe it.

Parashat Emor poses a challenge. It reminds us that there are things over which we have no control, most of which we will never be able to change. Not only the lower castes were trapped in their roles; so were the priests, who may have found it very difficult to fulfill the tasks they were assigned to do.

Parashat Emor asks us to practice a different kind of attentiveness: to agree to accept reality. As modern, free people, we believe we can change the way of the world, but I wonder if this is indeed necessarily so. And even if is, the quality of the process and the discourse vis-a-vis the desired change will be transformed and elevated if an element of deep acceptance is allowed. So, perhaps just for this upcoming Shabbat, can we consider accepting reality as is, before we try to change it?

Parashat Behar: The Lessons of Another Mountain

The mountain referred to in this week's parasha is Mount Sinai, but this drasha is based on a true story that happened on a different mountain - Massada – a few years ago.

It was 8 p.m., a beautiful night in the desert – not too hot, not too cold. Just perfect. I thought I smelled rain in the air, but it wasn't possible – it rarely rains on Massada. It must be the irrigation system.

Almost one hundred 6th graders from the Tali Tzafririm School in Hadera, accompanied by their teachers and parents, waited excitedly for the beginning of the night's unique program, all about heroism, idealism and big decisions. As the orientation sound & light show began, so did the lightning. The skies proved stiff competition for the dramatic film, as a spectacular lightning storm lit up the night skies. Looking back on the situation, I am amazed that I enjoyed that vision of Divine power, not seeing the flashes for what they were: warning signs of what was yet to come. But I had not listened to the weather report and I was absorbed in my task as educator of the group that night.

As the sound & light show provided by the Massada tourism site came to an end, we retreated to a quiet, sheltered spot to begin what was meant to be an absorbing story and discussion. God, however, had other plans. Tremendous winds began to blow and made continuing absolutely impossible, despite my best laid plans and years of experience at this particular site.

Realizing this week's parasha is Behar, and that it deals with Shmitta (i.e. letting go, releasing), I decided to take its message seriously and change the plan. Herding 100 children in the windy darkness took some time, but eventually everyone was settled in a large, snug tent. As the air became stuffy and my story progressed gradually to the suspenseful dilemma at its climax, rain began beating down noisily on the plastic tent cover, sending parents and children scrambling for their equipment outside and bringing my story to an abrupt and frustrating halt. How was I to make my educational point without completing it?

Once again I realized that I had absolutely no control, and let my well-laid plans go. The next step was for every child to read his or her drasha – carefully prepared over the past few months - to their parents. This emotional, meaningful ceremony turned into chaos as the powerful winds caused the electricity to go off and plunged us all into darkness.

The Assistant Head of the school was able to reach the Ministry of Education hotline on the phone in the office (all cell phone reception being cut off by the weather and location.) She was told that the rains were due to stop and we could continue our program in the morning.

Sleep, however, was not possible, due to the storm raging outside. By 4 a.m. it was clear that we would not be able to climb Massada as planned. The rain had not let up at all.

As the teaching staff debated whether to cancel the entire trip and write off what was supposed to be a transformative experience, together with the cost of its planning and aborted execution, I realized I had to make my own plans: I was expected at a Bar Mitzvah in Binyamina at 12 noon, many hours' drive away! My part of the event was meant to be over by 6 a.m. in any case, so I decided to start out earlier, allowing myself time to pull over and rest after the sleepless night.

As I began driving I saw that the road was strewn with rubble from the storm, in addition to small currents of water here and there. I approached a stronger current which was causing what seemed to be a minor flood on the road, and I decided to cross carefully, edging forward slowly until… the car came to a stop in the mud. I was completely stuck.

Never mind my beautiful new car – what about the Bar Mitzvah? There I was, alone on a remote road, in a rainstorm, in the mud. Surely my two hours of leeway would not be enough. Miraculously, I was able to make cell phone contact with the police station in Arad. After verifying with me that my life was not in danger, they politely asked me to wait for further instructions. I then called the school group to tell them not to begin the drive back, lest they, too, get stuck.

A return call from the Arad police station informed me that the road was completely blocked a little further up, that there was a minibus also stuck, and that they would not be able to reach me for several hours, during which I was not to get out of the car lest I get swept away in the current.

Suddenly, two Bedouins on donkeys rode by. Seeing my frustrated gaze as I registered the irony of being stuck despite my 21st century technology, the older of the two warned me not to stay in the car, in case a stronger current should carry it away. Who should I believe – the police, or this experienced dweller of the desert who had seen many such floods? And what about the sweet boy in Binyamina who was eagerly expecting me to officiate on this, his most momentous day?

For the third time, I decided to let go, לשמוט – I was not in control, and there was no use pretending otherwise. And so I did.

Immediately, a car with two younger Bedouins appeared, very pleased with themselves. They were amused by my predicament, but I no longer cared. The young men announced that they would rescue me and proceeded to plan. The rope they tied to my car snapped as soon as they began to pull it, but they did not give up. I put myself entirely in their hands. Once the car was finally out and they had been offered payment for their kindness (which they refused), they told me to drive behind them, as they knew how to navigate out of danger.

Although the car shook as we started out, I decided to reach the Bar Mitzvah ceremony first, and take it to the garage later. However, 200 yards up the road, we came to the minibus which was stuck there, and to the flooding the police had mentioned.

As I gave up all hope of performing a ceremony that day, a third Bedouin arrived in a jeep. His plan was not to pull the cars out, but rather to navigate them out by driving them himself, which he proceeded to do, much to my amazement. My no-longer-new car made it over sand, stones and slippery mud, looking much worse for the wear. My latest helper also refusing payment, I made my way to the nearest garage in Arad, where essential adjustments were made as I transformed myself in the restroom from a bedraggled, muddy traveler to an honorable officiating rabbi and then continued on my way, hopeful once again.

I arrived 45 minutes late, and although I was uncomfortable, having never been late to a ceremony before, I suddenly felt this was quite minor, in the grand, miraculous scheme I had witnessed. Feeling somewhat guilty for leaving the Massada group behind, I consoled myself with the thought that the miracle of my arrival made another significant rite of passage possible. And it was indeed a very significant and emotional event.

Parashat Behar begins like this:

"And the LORD spoke unto Moshe in Mount Sinai, saying: Speak unto the children of Israel, and say to them: When you come into the land which I give you, then shall the land keep a Sabbath unto the LORD. Six years you shall sow your field, and six years you shall prune your vineyard, and gather in the produce thereof. But in the seventh year shall be a Sabbath of solemn rest for the land, a Sabbath unto the LORD ... And you shall number seven Sabbaths of years unto you, seven times seven years; and there shall be unto you the days of seven Sabbaths of years, even forty and nine years... And you shall hallow the fiftieth year, and proclaim liberty throughout the land unto all the inhabitants thereof; it shall be a jubilee unto you; and you shall return every man to his possession, and you shall return every man to his family... for the land is Mine; for you are strangers and settlers with Me. For unto Me the children of Israel are servants; they are My servants whom I brought forth out of the land of Egypt: I am the LORD your God." (Vayikra 25)

My experience at Massada reminded me to take to heart a great lesson from this week's parasha: Shmitta, letting go! Man plans enthusiastically; he sows, reaps, grinds and sells; but he is not in control. He does not write the script of his life. Man and woman plan and God makes the wind blow and the rain fall whenever and wherever He chooses, even in May, in the desert.

Although my educational plan for the Tali group was disrupted, the real lesson was learned: "And freedom shall be proclaimed throughout the Land!" We should not delude ourselves – we are not in control, and therefore the commandment of letting go is truly freeing! We can only do our best, as we all tried to do that night on Massada. The rest is not up to us and never will be.

Parashat B'chukotai:
And None Shall Make You Afraid

We have finally reached the end of Vayikra.

Parashat B'chukotai - "In My laws" - says something very simple: if you follow my laws you will be blessed (the list of specific blessings is short and very sweet), and if you don't, you will be cursed. The list of curses is long, painful and cruel.

I have to admit: I truly believe in this paradigm. However, the parasha does not tell us which laws and commandments we must follow in order to be blessed. I am not at all sure that the famous 613 mitzvot are what is being referred to.

The curses are listed without pause, from minor to major, from difficult to horrific. As I read these I cringe, and hope that no one I know or love will experience even the lightest of them.

But as I observe human experience, I am stunned to see that most of humanity endures far more curses than blessings. Even those of us who are not physically deprived experience much of life through its hardship and difficulties. True, we don't consider ourselves cursed, but if asked to enumerate our blessings and curses, the script of our spontaneous thoughts would probably be a long list of pain, disappointment, fear, and competitiveness. You may think I am exaggerating, and that I am confusing curses with life's common challenges; or that we are just naturally accomplished complainers and whiners. I nevertheless insist that if one reads the list from a very broad perspective, perhaps even metaphorically (and I will not do that here), it does, indeed, reflect many of our common life challenges.

And if that is the case, what does this mean? Are our challenges and pain a punishment? And if they are, a punishment for what? Which laws did we ignore so completely that we deserve such punishment? Most of us are fairly decent people; we do our best, and try to be kind to ourselves and to others. Why should we experience so much pain?

At the end of the torturous list of curses, we find the following:
"Then shall the land be paid her sabbaths, as long as it lies desolate, and you are in your enemies' land; even then shall the land rest, and repay her sabbaths. As long as it lies desolate it shall have rest; even the rest which it had not in your sabbaths, when you dwelt upon it... then will I remember My covenant with Yaakov, and also My covenant with Yitzchak, and also My covenant with Avraham will I remember; and I will remember the land. For the land shall lie forsaken without them, and shall be paid her sabbaths, while she lies desolate without them; and they shall be paid the punishment of their iniquity; because, even because they rejected My ordinances, and their soul abhorred My statutes." (Vayikra 26:34-35, 42-43)

Incredible! Yet... very odd!

Is the point of exile to allow the land a thorough rest - i.e., to catch up on all the Shmitta years that hadn't been observed?

And if so, does the land have a will? Does the land want to rest every seven years - but we humans are unwilling to let it do so?

In the last chapter of Sayings of the Fathers it says: *"Exile comes to the world because of idol worship, incest, bloodshed and Shmitta."*

142

The first three are somewhat clear (or at least familiar to most of us), but why Shmitta? And what is the connection between the observance of Shmitta by human beings and the "will of the Land."

Last week we read about Shmitta for the very first time (in Parashat B'Har). Much has been said about the importance of the Shmitta, and how that importance connects it to Mount Sinai, to the giving of the Ten Commandments and the Torah itself.

Perhaps what makes Shmitta such a significant commandment (and its lack such a sin) is that it lies at the core of the human challenge! It carries the essence of our pain: Shmitta is the constant reminder to let go. Shmitta in Hebrew means very literally, to let go! Our inability to let go becomes our ultimate human sin.

The final curse then, is exile, galut. I would argue that human beings are indeed in exile. Our entire thought process testifies that we are disconnected from the world. Existentially we are in galut.

How so?

We all experience the world as an entity EXTERNAL to us – there is us and there is the world around us. This is the common human experience of the world. True, some people experience more of a connection with the world around them, but having a deep relationship with the world only further proves the point, that I and the world are separate entities, engaged is some kind of a relationship. This existential disconnect is the source of all of our fears (the world can be cruel), insanity (ISIS…), and pain (sickness and loss, for example).

We are so used to this existential fear that we may have never even thought about this quite this way. Well, you know, a fish in the water doesn't know it is wet, but it is...

And then, what do we do when our fears rise and threaten to drown or overwhelm us? We try (in vain, of course)) to control the crazy world - or at least the world closest to us. We do all we can to provide ourselves and our loved ones with a sense of security and safety. The illusion that we control our destiny helps us maintain our sanity. This is natural and human, and cannot be otherwise.

Animals are different. They don't have the frontal cortex of the mind. Their survival is in the here and now (or at most, extends to the coming winter). They don't try to control their environment; they just cater to their immediate needs. As far as we know, we are the only creature in Creation which tries to control both its environment and its future. This is a direct result of the deep sense of helplessness and fear that the knowledge of our impotence instills in us.

Our frontal cortex is both a blessing and a curse! A blessing, because it allows us to enjoy our advanced mental abilities! A curse, because our advanced brain tells us that we are separate from the world, and that the world is a dangerous place to live in. But we can do all kinds of things about it... and if only we control the world and tighten our grip on everything around us, we might just survive this life, this world...

Yet, we know - yes, deep inside we know - that we can't.

The parasha tells us that the Land "wants its Sabbaths"!
Indeed, Life "wants" to be lived.
Existence "wants" to exist.

The land "wants" to BE itself.

Hence, the opening words of our parasha: *"If you walk in My statutes, and keep My commandments, and do them"*, require of us that we let go of control (reminder: Shmitta = letting go in Hebrew). Furthermore, I would argue that the entire Torah and its commandments depend on our ability to let go, "Lishmot".

If we do, will everything be good? No! "Bad" things will continue to happen. One day we will not be here - both control freaks and carefree hippies. As Ecclesiastes said, our fate is the same.

So, by all means, we can and should save for a rainy day; we can and should plan well for our future. We should make sure we leave our loved ones with firm ground under their feet. But the most important thing we can and should do is to use our human consciousness - our frontal cortex - to understand that our personal survival is only a small part of the larger picture of creation, of the universe, of the "will of the land", of God.

Just as we honor our fears and concerns, we are also reminded to listen to the buzz of life itself, to creation's own desire to exist, to the land's longing to BE, and to the earth's womb-like ability to bear all forms of vegetation.

Perhaps this will also quiet our greed, soften our need for control, and our angst for ownership.

And then an amazing thing might happen: the pain, fear, and sense of exile will decrease, and we will suddenly feel the great blessing promised us in B'chukotai:

"...then I will give your rains in THEIR season, and the land shall yield HER produce, and the trees of the field shall yield THEIR fruit. And your threshing shall reach unto the vintage, and the vintage shall reach unto the sowing time; and you shall eat YOUR bread until you have ENOUGH, and dwell in YOUR land safely. And I will give peace in the land, and you shall lie down, and none shall make you afraid ... And I will walk among you, and will be your God, and you shall be My people. I am the LORD your God, who brought you forth out of the land of Egypt, that you should not be their bondmen; and I have broken the bars of your yoke, and made you go upright." (Vayikra 26:4-13)

Shabbat Shalom, a Shabbat of letting go, a Shabbat of sanity.

Parashat Bamidbar:
A Journalist's Point of View

This week we are beginning a new book – Bamidbar, In the Wilderness. The wilderness is the endless and unclear expanse in which we live each day. There are moments in which we experience clarity of vision, goals, and answers, but they are few and far between!

I recently heard an interview on the radio with Yonatan Berg, who is a journalist and a poet – a rare combination. Berg expressed this dichotomy between moments of clarity and daily confusion very well, hence his appearance in this drasha.

Berg spoke about his two professions: the journalist, who "knows" and reports, and the poet/artist who draws sustenance from the unknown, from the vast desert in which all that can be heard are the words of the Living God. Berg's professional interests reflect our own reality – living simultaneously in the world which is known and within our grasp, while accepting and being elevated by all that we don't know.

What was most exciting to me in this interview was that despite being such a complex (and at the same time very "normal") Jew, Berg has found HIS synagogue, i.e., HIS Jewish holy place. He describes the process of searching for that which would merge all of his yearnings: his need to be alone, on the one hand, and a desire to be part of a community, on the other; the craving for a spiritual anchor in the here and now, on the one hand, while remaining in the vastness of the Wilderness. I was moved to tears by this discussion, in a way that surprised me, especially as this confession came from a

147

currently non-observant person who has no halachic need of a formal commitment to synagogue life.

And so, as we approach both Bamidbar and the festival of Shavu'ot, I wish us all the ability to find that holy place (and may it be our synagogues), where we can all balance our journalist side which seeks facts (regardless of how actually true and precise they are), and the poet within us, who wanders in the wilderness as a person newly freed from Egypt, free of all definitive knowing, of binding logic, of limiting conditioning; free of the fear of the unknown that prevents most people from reaching the Promised Land.

In a few more parashot, in the middle of the book of Bamidbar, we will again meet these opposing characters – the journalist and the poet – in the form of the twelve spies who are sent to scout out the Land. Ten of these men bring back "facts," slightly altered by interpretation – as journalists do - which will cause panic, while the other two - Calev Ben Yefuneh and Yehoshua Binun – bring back the same facts, but they leave space for the unknown, for the poetic void, from which they draw strength and courage. Listening to Berg, I had the deep sense that it is there, in that union of opposites - of knowing and loving to know, and not knowing anything and surrendering to this lack of knowledge - that the keys to the Promised Land are hidden. These two men do, as we will see, enter the Land, while the other ten do not.

Parashat Nasso: It's Your Life - Carry it Carefully

I hope you had a good Shavuot festival, and that you received the Torah anew - fresh and refreshing as never before.

The theme of the week and the name of the parasha is Nasso. נ.ש.א. is the root of the verb that can be translated as **"carry", "lift",** or **"bear"**.

The parasha is very long, and it deals entirely with the meaning of this verb, and the way in which people **carry** or **bear** their lives. At the climax of the parasha, the priests are commanded to **lift** their hands up and bless the people of Israel with the wondrous blessing:
"May God bless you and protect you
May God shine His countenance upon you and be gracious unto you
May God lift His countenance to you and give you peace."

Several years ago a movie came out which left a great impression on me because it gave new meaning to God's advice to Cain, moments before the first murder is committed. The advice (unpunctuated and abbreviated) was "**If you are a more righteous person,** (you will be able to) **bear** (your burden). Most interpretations add the words in parenthesis in order to make sense of the words, and this works both grammatically and thematically. I read in this verse different advice altogether: "**If you bear** (your burden**) well**"... True, the sentence is not complete – there is no conclusion. I feel the conclusion is self-evident: if you **bear** your life well, then you are able to **bear** it well, and that is its own reward. There is, however, a warning as to what will happen if you don't: "And if you don't improve, wrongdoing awaits."

The movie was called "The Queen". It describes the events of the week following the tragic death of Princess Diana of Great Britain. Diana was beloved by the public, but a thorn in the side of the royal family. The movie shows the sense of general mourning, together with the reactions of two leaders – Prime Minister Tony Blair and Queen Elizabeth. Blair, depicted initially as young and dynamic in contrast to the sedate, conservative Queen, gradually seems superficial and rash, while the Queen's royal **bearing** becomes apparent. Blair's charm doesn't last the week of the movie, while the Queen's commands respect for the British Royal House and increases as the movie progresses. This is why she is Queen. Some of her subjects are frustrated by her apparent superfluity, and yet her task is simply to command respect.

In Israel the president (Nassi in Hebrew, from the same root under discussion) is the one who is expected to **carry** himself with dignity and to command respect for himself and for the entire nation. In our parasha, the heads of the tribes are called Nessi'im (presidents, or "those who **carry, bear** or **lift**") and they "**carry**" or "**bear**" sacrifices in honor of the consecration of the Tabernacle.

We are each born with a particular "deck of cards" – our family, the color of our skin, our genes, talents, handicaps and limitations, etc. No one explained why this is so or told us how best to play our "cards". Cain also doesn't get an explanation for the injustice he feels is done to him when his brother's sacrifice is accepted and his is not. He probably appealed to the heavens, saying "It's not fair!", but receives no Divine explanation. The only response he gets is "Right, life isn't fair, but if you **bear** it well..."

So everyone, welcome to the world. This is reality and this is the burden or the challenge: forgo any attempt to understand why life is so difficult for some, possibly even for the righteous, while for

150

others things have been so easy and smooth. The only thing we can do is exercise our total freedom to choose how well we **bear** or **carry** our reality.

The Levites in our parasha are required to **carry** the Tabernacle from place to place. This is their job. One of them may have **carried** a beautiful, shiny golden object, while another may have **carried** a dusty entrance mat. Such is life. The point is not what you **carry** but how you **carry** it, and especially who you become as you **bear** the burdens of your life.

There is some reward for our efforts hidden in the third line of the priestly blessing: (if you **bear** your life well, then)… "May God lift His countenance to you and give you peace."

Beha'alotcha: The Journey of a Lifetime

Parashat Beha'alotcha, the third in the book of Numbers, describes very precisely what happens to each of us when we embark on a great journey.

It begins with much anticipation. We sense an immense, forgotten light which was always there but has been covered by cobwebs and the dust of years. What is most amazing about this light is that enables us to see that everything is, in fact, One. Perhaps you have been lucky enough to sense that wonderful feeling that comes with the sudden realization that all is one, that everything is connected, that there is no real division between things, between people, or between nations.

The parasha opens with an experience of that Oneness - the festive lighting of the Menorah, the first in the history of the Jewish people. The Menorah is described with all of its ornamentation, molded entirely in one piece.

And then the first Passover festivities begin, exactly one year after the great Exodus. We have the first annual opportunity to renew our covenant of freedom, of our willingness to embark perpetually on a never-ending journey out of Egypt. Each time we experience the light which shows us that all is One, it is as though we are once again leaving Egypt. This perpetual process is like a spiral which returns to the same point with each circuit, slightly more elevated than the last. Our annual journey, marked in the month of Nissan, is one of rebirth and renewal.

Here we come to one of the great moments of grace in the Torah - a second chance is given to experience the Exodus. Two thousand years ago the Passover sacrifice was the main event of the holiday, but many people were ritually impure during the holiday so they were unable to partake in the ceremony. They turned to Moshe, asking for a solution, and he declared a second Passover date, a second chance. *"If any man of you or of your generations shall be unclean by reason of a dead body, or be in a journey afar off, yet he shall keep the passover unto the LORD; in the second month on the fourteenth day at dusk they shall keep it; they shall eat it with unleavened bread and bitter herbs."* (Sh'mot 9:10-11) If there were no second chances, would we be expected to be born and remain perfect, to see Oneness always? We are always whole, but we are not perfect. If we were, there would be no point in embarking on a journey.

Then, a moment before leaving the foot of Mount Sinai, last minute instructions are given to the People which will help them stay on course, as we all wish we could do.

The first is the sign which will show them the way: the cloud of God's presence lifting from the Tabernacle will be the sign to proceed. This may take some practice. In our own lives, when we realize we have spent too long at one point or other, it takes us time to absorb the fact that our current situation is no longer "it." We have learned all we can, and rather than continuing through inertia, it is time to follow the Cloud and find the next place in which to be deeply and fully present. We begin to understand that the Cloud will stubbornly, insistently, call us onwards and we must submit.

The second sign or instruction comes in the form of the blowing of the horns. Their sound creates a common language of urgent action, be it movement, pause, danger, or attention. Without this common language, a multitude cannot move together, and there is no community or nation. Each person would remain entirely on his or her own journey, or worse - unable to proceed at all.

And then, finally, after a very long and exciting stay at the foot of Mount Sinai, the People begin to move.

At this point an amazing thing happens. Moshe asks his father-in-law, Yitro (also called Re'u'el, meaning the Shepherd of God), to join the journey and help navigate. Yitro explains that he cannot, because it is not his journey!! Does this sound familiar? How we would love someone to take us by the hand and show us the way to our destination. Preferably, that person would also tell us what that destination is and why. But our lives are our own, and although they may seem very similar to other people's lives, they are also unique. Each person has his or her own Promised Land.

Yitro has given Moshe many gifts. He gives him bread and water when he is a young fugitive who has slayed an Egyptian; he gives him his daughter for a wife; he supports him and gives him advice on the division of leadership and the legal system. The last gift he gives, however, is perhaps the most significant. Yitro tells Moshe, "You are on your own life journey! Follow the Cloud, follow your God. Do not be tempted to follow a human advisor. I know this area very well, but I do not know the path of *your* journey."

As the People move forward, the difficulties surface almost immediately. They want meat. They are insatiable. (Does this sound like the Western world?) And then there is dissention within the leadership, with Miriam and Aharon speaking - perhaps jealously - about Moshe' wife. Miriam is smitten with leprosy and Aharon begs God for her to be healed, which she is. Only then does the journey continue.

154

This may seem an unlikely ending to this week's Torah portion, but it makes sense. The last incident is an example of what may take us away from our unique path. Our ego, our doubts, our fears, our desire to know and to arrive... All of these may present stumbling blocks and diversions, because it is hard to keep our eye on the Cloud and to devote ourselves to the unknown Divine within and around us, to trust and to submit.

So, my friends,
We embark (again) on a great journey, a journey of total dedication. As long as we move with the Cloud there is a very good chance that we will feel a deep, satisfying sense of oneness. The more we resist and argue, the more pain and frustration we are likely to experience. The choice is ours.

Parashat Sh'lach Lecha:
A Different Kind of Communication

Parashat Sh'lach Lecha brings us to the Negev. We have arrived at the edge of the Land of Israel! A year and two months have passed since the Exodus from Egypt and here we are! The Negev mountains are in the distance; the Promised Land is on the horizon.

But then God gives an odd order. He commands Moshe to send spies to scout the Land and return to report back to the People. Forty days later they return, very excited, full of impressions and wonder, and laden with the fruit of the Land. They all agree it is indeed a Land of Milk and Honey!!!

But then everything changes. The excitement turns into fear, and a huge argument ensues between ten spies who say that there is no chance of overcoming the mighty residents and fortifications of the Land, and the two spies who believe differently.

Who is right in this story? Who is telling the truth and who is not? Whom should we believe? Whom shall we choose?

Should we believe the ten spies who praise the Land but have no hope of attaining it? Is their report correct? Is their information accurate and objective, or emotional and affected by their fear? Are they friend or foe?

Or

Should we go with the two spies who agree with the facts presented by the other ten, but are the first in history to say (in Hebrew) "yes we can"? Are they right? Are they heroes or dangerous fools? Are they in terrible denial, or are they brilliant analysts?

We will never know. When Bnei Yisrael are told that they will not go into the Land and will die in the desert instead, they decide desperately to attack without leadership or organization. The results are disastrous! They are slaughtered by the resident nations and chased away. Only then do they accept the verdict: 38 more years of wandering, until the last of the generation of slaves dies. Perhaps the undisciplined attack proved that the ten spies are correct; that Bnei Yisrael ae not yet ready to inherit the Land.

At first the argument between the spies is factual and to the point. At the height of it, though, the Torah tells us that the ten spies: "... *spread an evil report of the land which they had spied out unto the children of Israel.*" (Sh'mot 13:32)

"Evil report" in Hebrew is "deeba". (Other translations are calumny, slander, and defamation.) The three-letter Hebrew root of deeba is ד.ב.ב., which has to do with encouraging one to speak (לדובב), and also dubbing, just like in English! At its root it does not connote negative or positive action. How, then, did it become synonymous with slander?

Similarly, the word for speech, whose root is ד.ב.ר. appears thousands of times in the Torah, usually in connection with God's words. "And God spoke to Moshe saying..." is a very common opening to biblical narratives. Even the word for wilderness, which is the physical space in which the Divine words are heard- מדבר - shares the same root.

But it goes even deeper. The art of speaking, of uttering words ("**diboor**") directly links a thing ("**davar**") with a speaker ("**dover**").

157

Dubbing or encouraging speech (deeba) is indirect. It turns reporting into interpreting; it implies encouraging or <u>interpreting someone else's speech</u>. Hence, deeba is inherently false, because it has the potential to misguide.

The twelve spies saw the Land, the real thing. Now they are standing in front of the masses, trying to convey their impressions. At first they are more precise in their description, but as they draw conclusions they begin to be less accurate - not only the ten pessimistic spies, but all twelve.

This is why the parasha is described as that of the "sin of the spies". Sin (chet, in Hebrew) means imprecision or that which misses the mark. This is a very common shortcoming, and it is why the most prevalent sin has to do with speech, gossip, or deeba (malicious talk). "Deeba" is essentially bad simply because it isn't the precise truth. Most of what we read in the daily papers is "deeba". Without exception, every paper specializes in the art of words whose connection to truth is tenuous at best. Unfortunately, there is no other way to report. The only true and precise voice is that of "a still small voice" (as God explains to Eliyahu in Melachim I on Mount Sinai), and that does not sell papers.

What would our journalism look like if we insisted on precise speech, as much as possible? What would our lives look like if we insisted on a conscious distinction between speech (dibur) and interpretation (deeba ד.ב.ב.), i.e. between what is accurate and what we think, feel or suggest?

I think our lives would be much easier, clearer, more serene, and the burden lighter if we stuck to the truth, because the truth is simple and unvarnished. I don't pretend to do so myself, yet. When and if I do, you will know, because I will be mostly silent!

We are the People of the Book, the People of the Word, the people who believe that the world was created through speech ("And God said … and it came to be"). The search for truth, which is the search for the conformance of a thing (davar) to a discussion of it (dibbur) is an integral part of our DNA. Perhaps this is the essence of our "chosenness". We were chosen (through words) to tell the world that it was created by speech; that the tongue is mightier than the sword! We are used to thinking of speech as a tool with which to describe reality. Yet the exact opposite is true: speech can create reality! As soon as the spies add their interpretation to what they saw, they create a new reality - one of fear, panic, and defeat.

So are they right? Of course they are, because they create a reality which did not exist beforehand. The information they give about the physical lay of the land is perfectly accurate, but in answer to the question – do we have the ability to inherit the land? -interpretation wins out, and with it the kingdom of lies, or slander.

None of us know the answer to the question. It is a spiritual one. If those same spies had gone on their mission in 1948 they would have returned to Ben Gurion of single mind: don't declare the State of Israel. Three years after the horrific Holocaust and in the face of tremendous threat from surrounding countries and the threat of an international weapons embargo, we didn't stand a chance. In fact, there were those who said as much. But Ben Gurion's vision worked. Not because his information was better, but because he decided that it would work. In the spirit of Yehoshua Bin-Nun and Calev Ben Yefuneh, the founders of the first Hebrew state decided *'We should go up at once, and possess it; for we are well able to overcome it.'* (Sh'mot 13:30). This was speech which created reality, our reality.

"The entire world is a very narrow bridge and it is most important not to fear at all." (R' Nachman). The truth, reality, is a very narrow bridge! Precision is the width of a needlepoint. All the rest is commentary, or דיבה (deeba).

Parashat Korach: For the Sake of Heaven

What a Torah portion! What a story! The first revolt against leadership from within the People of Israel. Korach the Levite and 250 of the top leaders rebel against Aharon's leadership,and through it , against Moshe.

The rebels have a very strong argument: *"and they assembled themselves together against Moshe and against Aharon, and said unto them: 'You take too much upon you, seeing all the congregation are holy, every one of them, and the LORD is among them; why then lift you up yourselves above the assembly of the LORD?'"* (Sh'mot 16:3)

Although their rhetoric is brilliant, their challenge is settled almost immediately in two miraculous ways: Aharon's staff magically blossoms, proving his right to lead, while the others' staffs remain unchanged - dry and lifeless; and then the earth opens up and consumes all 250 rebels!

As Korach's arguments seem legitimate and the dispute a worthy one, it is commonly interpreted as an example of a dispute that is "for the sake of heaven", as opposed to a dispute that is not "for the sake of heaven." Here is the quote from the Mishna, Pirkei Avot 5:17:

"Any dispute that is for the sake of Heaven is destined to endure; one that is not for the sake of Heaven is not destined to endure. Which is a dispute that is for the sake of Heaven? The dispute(s) between Hillel and Shamai. Which is a dispute that is not for the sake of Heaven? The dispute of Korach and all his company."

161

What does this mean? Each word and phrase of this quote is debatable, for example: Why dispute anything? What is "destined to endure"? I am particularly interested in the almost banal use of "for the sake of heaven", which is sometimes used to conceal a difficulty rather than to explain it.

What does "for the sake of heaven" mean?

Many people claim to be doing what they do "for the sake of heaven". What do they mean by this? Not for the sake of something else? For themselves? For their honor? Their country? What, (in "heaven's name"), makes it legitimate to say something is "in the name of heaven"? Who decides?

Usually the term is used to distinguish between something that is done from narrow self-interest, as opposed to… as opposed to what? Maybe for the sake of something more worthy? That answer seems too simplistic – we know that "heaven" is a term for something lofty and exalted, but we are no closer to understanding the distinction.

 Perhaps the way to measure whether there is an element of self-interest in one's actions is to check whether or not there is any form of monetary remuneration for one's deed. But what if the remuneration is not monetary, but one of self-esteem or honor? Is donating a kidney in order to feel righteous more or less worthy than selling it? The same recipient will benefit in exactly the same way.

What if one's sole intention in doing good is the joy of giving? Is that a form of remuneration? Does that make it not "in the name of heaven?"

In light of these questions, is it possible to say that there is nothing that is entirely for the sake of heaven? In other words, every action contains within it – consciously or unconsciously – the anticipation of gain, be it a sense of well-being, the calming of a guilty conscience, or giving meaning to our otherwise middling lives.

Our Sages and other commentators throughout the generations explained "for the sake of heaven" as "for the sake of uncovering the truth"; not to find justification for our own views, but rather to know what is true.

Although I am a follower of these wise men, I have to admit – I am not convinced!

I would like to suggest that ultimately, in essence, there is no real difference between "for the sake of heaven" and "not for the sake of heaven." This is because absolutely *everything* is *always* for the sake of heaven. The division under discussion here is a human distinction. That doesn't make it wrong or bad. It is even good, in a sense. Let me explain:

Our Sages say elsewhere that doing something with the expectation of benefit (i.e. perhaps not for the sake of heaven) is okay, because it will eventually cause us to act without expectation of benefit (for the sake of heaven). In other words, from our narrow, human perspective, we may think we are doing something for self-gain, but God created all creatures, and they (we) can *only* carry out His plan, His will.

If there are any exceptions to this, then God's power is limited. Perhaps He is not God at all, but just another power that exists in the world, one of many? The perception of God as a power among many that exist in our world is a very partial perception of God. Three times a day (morning, evening and before bed) we say "God is One". If this is so, then there can be nothing comparable. And if *this* is so – if All is One - then there is nothing a person can do that is opposed to God's will, and everything is "for the sake of heaven".

It's true that the Bible is full of examples of people going "against God's will" (take our current Torah portion, for example). But – following Rabbi Yehuda Halevi's ideas put forth his Kuzari book – these examples are all from and for a human perspective. Our limited consciousness makes it impossible for us to see the absolute, big picture. We create partial worlds in order to gain a sense of control and power, and to create logic in our lives.

And this is as it should be! Otherwise, we would blend into the grand scheme and lose our sense of right and wrong, of holy and profane, of good and bad. We need these measures in order to give structure and meaning to our human existence; to allow us to make choices – to choose what is right and life-giving.

Following this interpretation (and there are, as always, many others), the story of the demise of Korach and his supporters contains a moral which is there for human consumption: we strive to do good in our lives, while accepting God's decrees for what they are: beyond human understanding. There is something comforting in knowing that even our worst deeds may, at the end of the day, be for the sake of heaven, although at the time they seem the exact opposite. However, the challenge here is choosing to do good, even if right and wrong are human illusions and not Divinely true. There is tremendous value in this illusion, because it allows us to take responsibility to increase goodness in the world, and not to leave it up to God.

Three years ago at this time, we were mourning the brutal loss of three teenagers, sharing in the grief of their families. These amazing families have chosen to honor their sons' memories by actions that are right and life-giving, actions meant to unify and find common, human ground between Israelis of all walks of life and beliefs. They have chosen to turn their grief into a supreme example of creating meaning, while at the same time thoroughly accepting the notion of God's will being done in the world.

Parashat Chukat: The Ultimate Challenge

This Shabbat we read Parashat Chukat. The word "chuka" is the key to this Torah portion. It is translated as "statute", to distinguish it from other kinds of laws:

"This is the statute of the law which the LORD has commanded, saying.... And it shall be a perpetual statute unto them;" (Sh'mot 19:2-21)

This is not any statute – it is a statute commanded by God! This sounds promising – and then we discover it refers to the very confusing, odd, bizarre mitzvah relating to the ceremony of the Red Heifer: burning it, dissolving its ashes in water, and sprinkling on a person who has come into contact with the dead in order to purify him.

Confusing indeed! All the more so because it isn't just a mitzvah, it is a strongly worded "perpetual statute which the Lord has commanded." The traditional interpreters have various explanations, the main thrust of which is that the essence of belief is that a God-given command must be obeyed, regardless of whether or not we understand it. I find this explanation lacking.

Every week I ponder the upcoming parasha deeply as I go about my business. Its content colors my week as I await that "eureka" moment when a new insight makes its miraculous appearance. I find the sensation truly exhilarating.

And so it was this week – I looked and read and studied and thought and… nothing happened! Apparently a different approach is needed to this very challenging topic.

The parasha deals extensively with the issue of death. Not only purification from death, but the actual deaths - in the fullness of time - of the generation that has wandered in the desert for the last 38 years, including Miriam and Aharon. Others, who do not die of natural causes, are killed by a plague of poisonous snakes.

So the parasha is very much about transferring the flame from one generation to the next – from the generation that experienced the Exodus and Mount Sinai, to the generation that will enter the Promised Land.

This is a connection that can be made between the Red Heifer purification ceremony and the overall theme of the death. But it doesn't explain the reason for the ceremony, or the logic of one person becoming impure in the process of purifying someone else. (The slaughtering of the heifer renders the priest impure.)

And still – no eureka, no clarity, no bolt of lightning that I so look forward to each week. I am left with a huge riddle. I realize that the riddle isn't about the red heifer at all, but about death, the ultimate unknown, which casts its shadow on all of life as well. We draw comfort from the illusion of knowledge, the illusion of control.

Parashat Chukat reminds us the limits of our knowledge and control. We are being asked to accept this reality while maintaining a sense of curiosity and wonder, even as the generation that possesses more experience and seemingly more answers passes on.

The idea of a Red Heifer represents an ultimate goal, a time in which we can thoroughly accept life's wonders and mysteries. When this is achieved, the actual, unattainable Red Heifer will miraculously be found (perhaps on one of our kibbutzim) and it will herald the coming of Messianic Days (world peace? personal peace? The wolf lying down with the sheep? – each with his or her own dreams). In other words, any fulfillment requires deep understanding that is felt with one's entire being. When it is achieved, the challenge, obstacle or riddle that has seemed insurmountable is suddenly no more.

To quote Martin Luther King Jr and the prophet Yisha'ayahu:
"I have a dream that one day every valley shall be exalted, and every hill and mountain shall be made low, the rough places will be made plain, and the crooked places will be made straight; "and the glory of the Lord shall be revealed..."

Parashat Balak: A Blessing, After All

Parashat Balak tells us (once again) about the power of our will. Even God cannot, as it were, withstand human willpower. Just as He did not stop Cain from murdering Hevel; he did not stop Adam and Chava from eating from the Tree of Knowledge; he does not prevent horrific things from happening to blameless people each and every day. So in this week's parasha, He does not prevent Bil'am from setting out on a journey whose goal is to curse Bnei Yisrael.

My regular readers have no doubt noticed that there are several themes that appear throughout my drashot: human will, the human journey, the value of blessing, among others. These topics have interested me for years. Every person who comes to interpret the Torah will find topics in it that are of concern to him or her. We may not even notice the myriad other topics that the Torah addresses, even though every aspect of the human experience is to be found in it. In this way, a person has the opportunity for an intimate encounter with aspects of him or herself – week after week, year after year. And then, one day, he notices that the topic that has been occupying him for years has evaporated, and has been replaced by another. A new theme seems to leap forth out of the text and grab his attention. Another, new life-enhancing lesson awaits us. For now, the faithful kibbutznik in me is still dealing with the issue of personal will, versus that of the collective ideology of the kibbutz; the army officer in me is still attentive to orders from above; and the Zionist Jew in me is still committed to the calling of our national revival.

Here is a synopsis of the parasha: Balak, the king of Moav, bribes Bil'am, the regional pagan sorcerer, to come and curse Bnei Yisrael as they are travelling through his land on their way to Canaan. He wants them to be weakened, so that Moav can do battle against them and chase them out of their country. Bil'am is a pagan sorcerer, but he is God fearing! He listens to Him and insists on communicating only with the Divine voice. On the face of it, it would seem that Bil'am is very righteous. Why, then, do the Torah and the Sages consider him to be such a scoundrel?

Bil'am is much like you and me. Just like him, we want things, we may even want them very badly, even when we know that God, our conscience, or our common sense tells us specifically "no!" Perhaps it is not good for us; for society; for the world; for our health, and perhaps it is just not for the highest good. Yet we cannot seem to resist.

The ancient Hebrew commandment, long before any other commandments existed, was, "And you shall be a blessing...", and then "through your descendants all the nations of the earth will be blessed..." For that which brings blessing to the world is Divinely blessed, and will forever be blessed. Even though "in every generation there are those who rise up against us to destroy us..." (as we read in the Haggadah).

God's blessing to Avraham and his descendants is not a personal one! It does not say anything at all about us as individuals. Avraham's life was very difficult, as were Yitzchak's and Yaakov's (who even said so to Pharaoh).

The blessing says that the journey of life – that eternal movement of God in the world which brings Creation into being every day anew, and redeems everything that has been enslaved into freedom – that movement is a blessed one; a journey towards blessing; a journey which has been divinely decreed to be for the ultimate good.

One can try to hijack this Divine movement of life, use it and abuse it. Many have tried - all those who have tried to enslave Jewish or human creativity are guilty of that. A strong personal desire for greed and power may temporarily get its way, but not for long. It will not withstand the tremendous power of the wheels of divine evolution. Ultimately, nothing can withstand the Heavenly will to pour blessings into creation. The giant wheels of LIFE will turn. They will turn for goodness and they will turn for blessing.

This is just the way it has to be.

May it be your will, our God and God of our Forefathers and Mothers, that our will align with yours. May the disparity between our will and Yours be reduced, so that our deeds will bring blessing to the world which You create every day anew. May our deeds strengthen life and not weaken it.

Parashat Pinchas: Our Delightful Sins

"For there is not a righteous man upon earth that does (only) good and never sins." (Ecclesiastes 7:20)

We all have our own personal, God-given sins. They are part of Creation, and **they, more than our righteous deeds, enable our own existence and continuity.**

Twice in Parashat Pinchas there is reference to this radical notion of inevitable sin. In both cases it relates to the final reckoning of a person's life.

The first instance is that of Tzlofchad. He dies and leaves no sons to inherit his portion in the Promised Land. His daughters demand to inherit their father's ancestral-land-to-be. They tell Moshe that their father was not one of Korach's company, and therefore his death is not because of that sin: *"Our father died in the wilderness, and he was not among the company of them that gathered themselves together against the LORD in the company of Korach,* **rather, he died in his own sin;** *and he had no sons."* (Numbers 27:3)

His own sin?
What does this mean?

The classic interpreters emphasize the distinction between what can be attributed to Tzlofchad alone, and the sins for which many others died (the Golden Calf, the "graves of greed", Korach and his company, the spies and their supporters, and those who lusted after the women of Moav and Midian. There is no lack of fatal sins during the wilderness journey. So, now we know which sins were **not** Tzlofchad's, but why does the text say "**he died in his own sin?**"

The second case referring to one's inevitable sins occurs a little later in the parasha: *"And the LORD said to Moshe: Ascend unto this mountain of Avarim, and behold the land which I have given to the children of Israel. And when you have seen it, you also shall be gathered unto your people, as Aharon your brother was gathered; because you rebelled against My commandment in the wilderness of Tzin, in the strife of the congregation, to sanctify Me at the waters before their eyes. These are the waters of Meribath-Kadesh in the wilderness of Tzin."* (Numbers 27:12-14)

Moshe does not have a memory problem. Why, then, is he being reminded of his sin? Perhaps the issue is not Moshe's memory, but our own. Besides, we don't actually know what Moshe's sin was. The Sages are divided over this question - was it his wrath with the Children of Israel? Was it that moment of possible arrogance as he gathered the people? Was it indeed the fact that he struck the rock instead of speaking to it? Was it because he struck twice, and not once? We don't know, just as we don't know what Tslophchad's sin was!

The Torah may want to remind **us** that the details are unimportant - they are pure gossip. What is important is that every person sins. No one is without sin. Our Bible reminds us of this over and over. Not one of the biblical heroes are without sin: Adam and Chava, Cain, Enosh, Noach, the descendants of Shem, Cham and Yefet, Avraham, Sarah, Yitzchak, Rivka, Yaakov, Leah, Rachel, Reuven, Yoseph, Yehuda, Miriam, Moshe, Aharon, Shaul, David, Shmuel, Shlomo, and so on…

Arrogantly, we think we know what the sins of all of the giants of our heritage were. But in fact, if we really read closely, perhaps with the help of our Sages, we will discover that we don't, just as we don't know anything about Tzlofchad's very own personal sin, other than: **"he died in his own sin."**

The famous poet Zelda wrote: "Each of us has a name, given by our sins and given by our longing." (The full translation can be found at the end of the drasha.) Zelda makes the connection between a person's name, his sins and his longing, because every person does, in fact, sin.

We all so much want to do what is right. We so much want to be righteous, and it doesn't work, because it can't.

The immediate connection between sin and death appears early in the Torah. Adam and Chava are warned not to eat from the Tree of Knowledge and from the Tree of Life lest they die. And indeed, they eat from the Tree of Knowledge, their eyes are opened, and they become conscious of mortality and death.

From this story on, there is an awareness of death in the world, and this awareness is linked to sin. Christianity calls it "original sin", and it became synonymous with human weakness, blindness and insignificance. It also is used in reference to all things sexual, and is used to judge (and damn) women's sexuality.

Not so in the Jewish tradition! This is a very basic difference between Judaism and Christianity. While Judaism, too, considers the act of eating from the Tree of Knowledge a sin, it considers it essential to the grand scheme of Creation. With awareness comes the acknowledgement of separateness, which is the point at which human history begins. It is through the awareness of separateness

174

that a relationship between me the world is created. All relationships, all intimacy, all love, all longings, go back to that life-enhancing sin.

When Adam and Chava make this discovery, they cover their nakedness. They discover individuality, and with that, they also discover mortality.

Every time we utter words like "I", or "me", the Tree of Knowledge speaks from deep within us. Our defiance of God is repeated each time we refer to ourselves as individuals. Yet, that same primordial defiance (also known as sin) is the key to all human creativity and all of human accomplishments.

And yes, it is the source of each and every sin that will follow.

Hence, this defiance is both a source of strength and achievement, and a source of suffering. We struggle to maintain our individual "I"-ness, although without it life would be so much easier. But it would not be ours!

We can change Descartes' famous quote, "I think, therefore I am," with: "I exist, therefore I sin."

Tzlofchad, the father of those five daring women, lived and died as we all do: with an identity, which is why his daughters want to claim HIS land. In reality, no land is HIS, or MINE. But in reality, we all pass on the seeds of the fruit of the tree of individuality. We all educate our offspring to celebrate that primordial, painful, and life-enhancing sin.

Moshe, though a great prophet, was mortal, and therefore he, too, had to die "in his own sin." If he didn't, he might have become some kind of divine being. As he stood by the rock of the water of life and struck it, he essentially declared... "I"! And indeed life-giving waters came pouring forth.

There is something comforting about this idea. It allows us to come to terms with our humanity, with our human imperfections and sins, which are all related to the survival of our "I"-ness. Without them, there would be no love in the world, no creation, no joy. True, there would also be no death, but this is a package deal.

You, too, ate from that tree. So, "BE"! Be human! Embrace your uniqueness! For through your very own I-ness you will get to know God. Guaranteed.

EACH OF US HAS A NAME / ZELDA

Each of us has a name
given by God
and given by our parents

Each of us has a name
given by our stature and our smile
and given by what we wear

Each of us has a name
given by the mountains
and given by our walls

Each of us has a name
given by the stars
and given by our neighbors

Each of us has a name
given by our sins
and given by our longing

176

Each of us has a name
given by our enemies
and given by our love

Each of us has a name
given by our celebrations
and given by our work

Each of us has a name
given by the seasons
and given by our blindness

Each of us has a name
given by the sea
and given by
our death.

© Translation: 2004, Marcia Lee Falk
From: *The Spectacular Difference*
Publisher: Hebrew Union College, Cincinnati, 2004

Parashat Matot-Masa'ei:
Finding Beauty, Because It's There

This week we end the book of Bamidbar (In The Wilderness, or "Numbers" in English) with a double portion of beauty: Matot-Masa'ei.

Matot details some of the final instructions given to Bnei Yisrael at the tail end of their forty-year-long journey. These instructions concern the power of the spoken word and of oaths. The parasha then completes the story of Israel vs. the Midianites, with Pinhas leading the Israelite war of revenge against the people who tried to "steal" Israelite hearts. In Matot God defines the ultimate boundaries of the Promised Land, but then two tribes express their preference for the good and lush land outside of the Land of Israel, and ask Moshe not to cross the Jordan River into the Promised Land. Surprisingly, Moshe agrees, on the condition that they will assist their brethren in conquering the Land, which they do.

The second parasha, Masa'ei was originally the last in the Torah, before an additional, summarizing book – D'varim - was added. Masa'ei, means "voyages of", and it summarizes the entire journey of the People of Israel from Egypt until this point. The journey begins with the Exodus from a narrow, confining place (Tsar, Mitsrayim), and ends a moment before reaching the Promised Land. This is the nature and essence of *every* journey! The 42 stops referred to in the text parallel 42 milestones in the life of each and every one of us – some internal, some external.

All 42 milestones are "resting points" (חניה). Between each resting point there is a journey. Some of the resting points are pleasant, while others are very demanding. Some sustain while others challenge us. The secret of knowing when to journey and when to rest, when to make a move, when to stay put - for a few hours or for many years – is decided, in the Torah and in our lives, by the Divine Cloud.

The word "chanaya" means, encampment, stopping point, parking or dwelling place, both in ancient and in modern Hebrew. The actual word in the Parasha is "Vayachanu" (and they encamped). As mentioned, this word appears 42 times in the course of Israel's journey! Vayachanu contains the word "Chen", meaning beauty, grace, favor or charm. One way of viewing and evaluating the journey, then, is by the degree of "chen" to be found in each place, the implication being that the Israelites dwelled longer in places where they found beauty, favor, or grace. The two letters in the word "chen" also create the word Noach, which means comfortable and restful. So the encampments were places of rest, of comfort, of beauty, and of grace. However, in spite of all these synonyms, every resting point comes to an end –natural or forced. Either way, when the "Chen" ends, the Cloud lifts and it is time to move on.

We are all too familiar with the chapters of wandering in the Jewish story of persecution. This week we are asked to look at the moments of rest, beauty, and grace - as individuals and as a People. "Chen" challenges us to STOP and sense what in Creation is good and nourishing.

A non-Jewish newcomer from North America pointed out to us recently how hectic our lives are! He said that "you Jews don't ever stop!" He didn't mean this in a negative sense, just as an observation. (Perhaps it takes a hyperactive people to bring the gift of the Sabbath to the world.)

How then do we stop? How do we create a Chanaya? From the Hebrew language we learn that resting and stopping requires an acceptance of "enough". The word for enough is די (Dai). Dai is both the root of the word Todah (gratitude) and Yehudi (Jewish)! Leah named our forefather, Yehudah, after whom we are named, when she finally STOPPED trying to win over Yaakov's heart. Instead she THANKED God for what she has, and said ENOUGH. Enough! - Chen informs us – nothing needs improving! Enough! – Chen tells us – there is enough, and you don't need more!

This is no easy task. It takes practice. Hence we get 42 opportunities.

The great teacher Jeremiah, who prophesied at a very difficult time in our history and whose words we will read and lament over on Tisha B'Av next week - said: *"Thus said the LORD: the People who escaped from the sword have found CHEN [beauty] in the wilderness; God has come to comfort Israel."* (Jeremiah 31:1)

Nothing has changed. We are the People who constantly escape the sword. We are the People who have seen the deadly end of the sword repeatedly throughout our history. No wonder we are hectic, ambitious, constantly seeking more.

But, the Parasha tells us, we all need times of Chen. No journey is complete without it.
We are the People who invented the term "Tikkun Olam". 21st century Jews love this term. I am embarrassed to say (so I will whisper), that I don't! "Tikkun Olam" implies that the world is a broken place. That it requires fixing. That it is flawed. I know, most of you will now say: "Nu!... is that not true? Is that not self-evident???? Just look at the Middle East, the real Middle East – Syria, Iraq, etc. Gevalt! The world has gone Meshugane. And what makes it even more broken, is that they end up blaming us for it..."

We have learned that we can't trust anyone to protect us, and sometimes it seems like we can't even trust God! We are not the nation that printed "In God We Trust" on its bank notes! We do the opposite: we amass wealth because we don't trust – not the Fed, nor God!

Jews have a recognized ability to fix and improve. We have won many noble and Nobel prizes for it. But once in a while, just once in a while, we are asked to STOP, REST, OBSERVE, focus on what is (already) favorable, what works beautifully, what is already good in everything! After all, before we fled the sword, we taught the whole world that all that God created was good. Even "very good"! Do we still stand by the teaching we delivered? Can we imagine Tikkun Olam starting not with the assumption of the brokenness of the world but with a calling to see the radical goodness that permeates God's creation? I know… some of you are rolling your eyes and saying: "there goes another naïve liberal hippie." I will take that risk! I have God and Torah on my side.

Farewell Wilderness. The Promised Land has never been closer; never been lovelier!

Parashat D'varim, Shabbat Hazon: Finding Grace

This week we begin a new book, the fifth and final book of the Torah, D'varim.

Last week I wrote about the root ‎ח.נ. in reference to the 42 stops the Israelites made on their desert journey. I explained that "Chen", can also mean beauty, grace, favor or charm, and we looked at how stopping and viewing the "chen" in our surroundings can be life-altering.

This week we will look at the same word in a different context.

As the book of D'varim opens, Moshe is standing in front of Bnei Yisrael, in front of a new generation which did not know Pharaoh, and he is teaching them the secret of entry into the Promised Land. Moshe reviews the history of Bnei Yisrael thus far, including a (completely revised) story of the twelve spies. (As we know, the punishment for that collective sin was a lengthening of the journey by 39 years, and the end of the generation of the Exodus. Only those born in freedom in the desert will be allowed to enter the Promised Land.)

Here is what it says:
"Moreover your little ones, that you said (that you worried, upon entering the Land) *should be prey, and your children, that this day have no knowledge of good or evil, they shall go in there, and to them will I give it, and they shall possess it."* (D'varim 1:39)

Wow! Adam and Chava eat from the Tree of Knowledge Good and Evil and are banished from the Garden of Eden. And here, the children of those who left Egypt, who have no knowledge of good or evil, will enter the Promised Land! Does this mean that knowledge of good and evil **banishes** from Eden, and lack of such knowledge **enables** entry into the Promised Land? Are we supposed to shy away from ethical behavior? Should we stop trying to do good in the world? Should we ignore the world of values we learned from our parents and impart to our children?

Of course not!

Tomorrow night we will mark the beginning of Tisha B'Av. Five tragic events occurred on this date according to our Sages, among them the destruction of the First and Second Temples, the sin of the twelve spies, and the punishment imposed on Bnei Yisrael not to enter the Land and to perish in the desert.

The twelve spies who tour the Land are amazed by its abundance and say it is a Land of Milk and Honey. But then, ten of the spies begin to slander the land. How can this be? Did they change their minds? We are all familiar with conversations that go like this: "She is so talented! And she's beautiful, and a great mother, but…" And then we hear a long, lethal pronouncement that banishes all the good we heard previously.
Tradition has it that the Temples in Jerusalem were destroyed because of needless hatred. We repeat this mantra over and over whenever we wish to condemn the actions or speech of another. It always seems to be the other person's fault, never our own…

In Hebrew the word translated here as "needless" is "chinam", meaning free, or without cost, which can be understood as "without reason." But we always feel there is a reason!

Another meaning of the world "chinam" may be the key to a different understanding of the phrase and of both the destruction and the sin of the spies. "Chinam", as we saw in the previous parasha, also means "their grace" or "their charm". Hating another person's behavior is something we understand. But hating another's grace is an entirely different story. This is a case of jealousy, pure and simple. A person's grace is their light. In terms of good and evil, grace is all that is good in a person. In a sense, this is hatred of that which is divine in the other, that which is unique and amazing about him or her.

When one hates the grace, the light and beauty in someone or something, it does not leave any room for redemption or repair. Hating an evil or ugly act is entirely understandable, but hating the grace is pathological; it can cause a snowball effect, so that destruction – even a small-scale one within friendship, family or work relations - becomes a forgone conclusion.

The opposite of hatred without reason is, of course, love without reason. Knowing how to love the grace in another person is a wonderful ability! It begins consciously, and inevitably leads to love. And then a miraculous thing can happen – that snowball of love can begin to roll back up the slippery slope! This would not normally be possible based on the laws of nature, but it is definitely possible in the case of loving without cause. Layers of heavy ice can shed gradually, until all that is left is the original grace which God created and which is present a moment before the story of the Tree of Knowledge, when God says "And it was good." Divine good, the grace of Creation, the light that is hidden in the depths of all that is, **is there for anyone who is willing to see it.**

Moshe is standing in front of Bnei Yisrael, in front of a new generation which did not know Pharaoh, and he is teaching them that it is not knowledge of good and evil that banishes, but rather being judgmental! In reality there are no grades, no judgment. Reality is full of grace. Open your eyes differently; look with new eyes that do not seek good and evil, seek the grace that is in all things. Follow it, seek it, and loving will happen naturally.

I do not mean to imply that this is easy to do – it isn't! This is not a quick course in finding one's ability to love. Being able to see the grace in another and in creation requires recognizing the grace within us and feeling at peace with it. Otherwise, jealousy, based on the fear of being unworthy, will poison our vision.

The prophet of destruction who saw us in our ugliest hours wrote Megillat Eicha. He is also the one whose words will console us at the end of Tisha B'Av:
"Thus said the LORD: the people who were left of the sword have found grace in the wilderness, even Israel, whom I go to console."
(Jeremiah 31:1)

Parashat VaEtchanan:
When Moshe Truly Reached the Promised Land

Tish'a B'Av has passed – we can breathe again! Today is Tu B'Av, the Jewish Valentine's Day, so love, rather than mourning, is in the air.

The Shabbat following Tish'a B'Av is called Shabbat Nachamu, taken from the first words of this week's Haftorah. But the Parasha is Parashat VaEtchanan.

Once again the issue of Moshe's entrance into the Promised Land is under discussion. This time, though, Moshe is telling Bnei Yisrael that he actually pleaded with God to enter! Up until this point we are not 100% sure of Moshe's response to God's decree – Moshe may have been relieved (after all, he never wanted the job in the first place and asked to quit several times); perhaps he is quietly resigned, accepting God's plan with grace; perhaps he is angry and hurt. But in Parashat Vaetchanan the matter is made clear: Moshe is pleading to cross the Jordan and see the Land up close. The parasha is even named after his plea (va-etchanan means "and I pleaded").

Once again we are filled with sorrow for this man who dedicates his life to the journey to Eretz Yisrael and dies a moment before entering it. This appears to be the ultimate tragedy.

On the other hand, another voice pipes up and wonders: Sorrow? Really? Perhaps this was a supreme act of Divine kindness! After all, someone has to tell us when to quit, when we have done enough and can finally rest.

Yet Moshe is really pleading!! Can't he just enter, kiss the holy ground and then die? Why abuse a person who dedicates his life to the cause of the People and the Land? Even Ben Gurion, shortly before his passing, got to see the Old City and to hear the famous declaration "The Kotel is in our hands", after losing it to the Jordanians in 1948. Even Golda got to meet Anwar Sadat in Jerusalem after the horrendous Yom Kippur War, a war for which she was held partially responsible.

This year I would like to suggest another reading of this seemingly-familiar text. It will involve close reading, and I will add my comments to make my point clear.

First, let us return to the plot of Deuteronomy/D'varim. This last and final book is a collection of Moshe's parting speeches to Bnei Yisrael prior to his death. In our parasha there is a three-way conversation taking place between Moshe, God and Bnei Yisrael. I am "hearing" a shockingly new idea in this "trialogue." It was never apparent to me before, I must admit. Moshe's plight is often seen as a punishment for hitting the rock instead of speaking to it to draw forth water, but this is not actually stated in the text. The "real" reason remains unknown; hence it is open to interpretation. Here is the text:

"And I pleaded with the LORD at that time, saying: 'O Lord GOD, You have begun to show Your servant Your greatness, and Your strong hand; for what god is there in heaven or on earth that can do according to Your works, and according to Your mighty acts? (As you are so mighty, why should it bother you -) *Let me go over, I pray You, and see the good land that is beyond the Jordan, that goodly hill-country, and Lebanon.' But the LORD was wroth with me for your sakes* (for your sakes?)*, and hearkened not to me; and the LORD said to me: 'Let it suffice you; speak no more to Me of this*

187

matter. (Enough already!) *Get you up into the top of Pisgah, and lift up your eyes westward, and northward, and southward, and eastward, and behold with your eyes; for you shall not go over this Jordan. But charge Joshua, and encourage him, and strengthen him; for he shall go over before this people, and he shall cause them to inherit the land which you shall see.' So we abode in the valley over against Beth-Peor.*

"And now, O Israel (now that we have made this point clear), *hearken unto the statutes and unto the ordinances, which I teach you, to do them* (how exactly does this connect to the rest of the story?); *that you may live, and go in and possess the land which the LORD, the God of your fathers, gives you. You shall not add to the word which I command you, neither shall you diminish from it* (Nothing may be changed? This seems rather extreme, certainly "not Jewish"), *that you may keep the commandments of the LORD your God which I command you. Your eyes have seen what the LORD did in Baal-Peor; for all the men that followed the Baal of Peor, the LORD your God has destroyed them from the midst of you.* (Why exactly are we suddenly being reminded of this episode?) *But you that did cleave unto the LORD your God are alive every one of you this day."* (Deuteronomy 3-4)

So… What is so shocking, you may be wondering.

We are all so sure that the journey is from point X to point Y, from Egypt to Canaan, from the desert to the Land of Israel, from exile to the Promised Land. And yet here is Moshe, the captain and leader of this great voyage, being prevented from completing the journey. He begs and pleads to reach the finish line, and God is "wroth" and says "let it suffice".

As we know, not only does Moshe's life story end on the "other" side of the Jordan, so does the entire Torah!

In the past I have alluded to the notion that it is the journey that counts and not the arrival. Now I would like to suggest a different option: God is telling Moshe here that the entire human understanding of time and space is basically incorrect. The notion that we are meant to complete a certain life journey, with X achievements (degrees, years of study, economic status, number of children, etc.) in Y years is entirely erroneous. Many in their 40s, 50s, and 60s indeed wonder what have they accomplished. Have they accumulated enough certificates to prove their worth? Have they wasted their time? So many reach their 70s mired in endless regrets over what appear to be mistaken choices and omissions.

Time and space – two deceptive dimensions which are the cause of endless misery!
Is there necessarily a journey from X to Y?
Is the distance between X and Y measurable? Is it permanent and objective?
Is there a recommended or expected time in which to go from X to Y?

Most people would say "Of course there is! Of course, after all, space is measurable, objective and permanent. If one knows the speed of movement it is possible to calculate precisely how long it will take to get from one point to another." But this obvious truth has never been proven! Our senses tell us "of course" - the Swiss timepiece and the odometer will prove it - but this proof is only phenomenological, dependent on our senses which are, at best, not entirely reliable. We know that our sense of time and space are very subjective and that there is no ontological, logical, or philosophical proof of their existence.

The Torah is nearing completion. Until now it has been fairly linear regarding time: it begins with the stories of Creation (10 generations), Noach and the flood (another 10 generations), Avraham, Yitzchak and Yaakov, Yoseph going to Egypt, Bnei Yisrael as well (covering 5 generations). Two hundred years later they are enslaved. Then Moshe is born, and we he turns 80 they are freed and return home (another 40 years). The Torah has also been linear in terms of space: Go forth from your land and your birthplace... to the land that I will show you; go down to Egypt; go to Haran; climb up this mountain; encircle the land... etc.

D'varim is the last chance for God to teach Moshe a new Torah, and for Moshe to teach it to Bnei Yisrael. This "New" Torah is a non-linear one. Not only is God unconcerned with the destination, He isn't even interested in the journey! He's actually not concerned about anything at all, He just Is – now, in the present, hence God's name selected by Him after the Exodus: HaVaYaH (which means "being" or "in the present"). All the rest – the dimensions of time and space through which we perceive our existence – are a wondrous invention of the human mind. They are not an illusion, they are our creation.

When God is "wroth" with Moshe for his request, perhaps he is really saying: Enough! Get out of your limited human grasp of time and space! How many times do I have to tell you there is no place to get to! Go up the (figurative) mountain, to the higher spheres of being and see – you are already there! As soon as you realize this you will simply Be in a different, truer dimension. As long as a person lives within time and space he or she is trapped by them and by the desire to reach something, to be elsewhere. One can never be content because "I haven't been there yet, I haven't accomplished this or that yet...." As soon as you learn, Moshe, that there is no such thing, you will become... eternal. Moshe, you are already exactly where you are supposed to be. You are in your place. This is why

190

another key name for God is "HaMakom", The Place. God alone is the destination, the place, and He is right here, right now, always.

In this parasha Bnei Yisrael are encamped opposite Beit Pe'or. (Pe'or is similar to the word "pa'ar", which means "gap".) They are encamped in the gap ("pa'ar") between the now and the later, between who I am and who I would like to be, between who I think I am and who others think I am. This is the nature of our lives. The effect of these gaps is constant and upsetting. Pe'or of the Bible is a well-known idol of the region. So is the feeling of division that the perceived gaps create in our lives. These gaps are idolatrous in that they stand in radical contrast to God's Presence or Being, which is the real Promised Land.

This is why Moshe continues his speech by saying "go in God's path, not in that of Pe'or. See how all those who followed Pe'or died. That path always leads towards death. If you are here in the present, in the Place, you are truly alive."

The final verse of this speech is *"But you that did cleave unto the LORD your God are alive every one of you this day."* Alive! This day!

It is not an act of kindness that God does to Moshe in not letting him cross over the Jordan, and certainly not a punishment (I don't believe there are punishments in the Torah, only repercussions). It is God saying to Moshe, "Enough with this crossing business! You are already here, you are present. You always were. Now you can rest. You have reached the Promised Land. You were always there, but because you were not aware of it, it is as if you were not yet there. As for Bnei Yisrael, let them cross the Jordan. They are still trapped in the dimension of Pe'or. So is Joshua. This is why he must continue to lead them. You, who have arrived, cannot teach them anything else." And you? Where are you?

Parashat Ekev: The Time is Now

Ekev means "as a result". This is the theme of this Parasha: "If... then..." In philosophy this is called Determinism: cause and effect. Every phenomenon has a reason, and every reason has a reason behind it and so on.

Aetheists will say that this chain is never-ending, that there is no originating source. The Theist philosophy (that of those who believe in the existence of a Creator, a Supreme Power, God) can accept the idea of Determinism, but they will insist that there is, indeed, an original impetus called Creation.

Based on this idea, Parashat Ekev (the parasha of Determinism) tells us what will bring blessing to the world (if... then...) and what is the ultimate sin (if not...) and its price (then...).

The sin referred to in Parashat Ekev is the essence of all sins, represented in the Torah by the generation of the Tower of Babel, the Golden Calf, the sin of the spies, Korach and his company, the sins that brought about the destruction of the Temples, etc. And since the Torah is our own eternal, personal story, these are the essence of our own sins.

Here is the text:
"Beware lest you forget... lest when you have eaten and are satisfied, and have built goodly houses, and dwelt therein; and when your herds and your flocks multiply, and your silver and your gold is multiplied, and all that you have is multiplied; then your heart be lifted up, and you forget the LORD your God, who brought you forth out of the land of Egypt, out of the house of bondage; who led you through the great and dreadful wilderness, wherein were serpents, fiery serpents, and scorpions, and thirsty ground where was no

water; who brought you forth water out of the rock of flint; who fed you in the wilderness with manna, which your fathers knew not… and you say in your heart: 'My power and the might of my hand has gotten me this wealth.'"(Deuteronomy 8:8-17)

This, in a nutshell, is the essence of human sin: we forget that we are actors and not the director. We are sure that we took ourselves out of Egypt, out of the narrow places in our lives; that we built our homes and filled up our bank accounts; that we increased our possessions, found water in the desert (and today we can even desalinate it).

Are we wrong? Of course not! All of modernism is based on this notion. This is the goal of our educational system, the source of our values. This is how we are judged by the OECD. Only when we managed to release ourselves from the tyranny of the religious worldview described in Chapter 8 of Deuteronomy did the creative periods such as the Renaissance, the Industrial and Scientific Revolutions take center stage in history. Modern man was free to engage in his and her pursuits, and human accomplishments soared.

We teach our children that "he who tries succeeds", that eating well and exercising will make us healthy, that he who prepares for Shabbat will eat on Shabbat… So why shouldn't we take the credit? We deserve it! The Enlightenment freed us from our chains by releasing us from the bondage of religion. What has sin to do with anything? It is time to rid ourselves from such outdated nonsense!

Yet even in the Bible and in the books that followed it, these well-known "sins" are also the source of great achievement: the Tower of Babel was an engineering masterpiece; Korach's battle was for democracy; the edifice complex of our parasha led to the building of the two Temples, Caesarea, and Herodion – all major architectural accomplishments admired throughout the Roman world. And yet…

193

I still insist that the sin described in Chapter 8 is The Sin, not to be confused with "the sin." It contains both the secret of human development, and the source of all human suffering. How can this be reconciled - the sin of pride, alongside the secret of human accomplishment?

The answer lies, as it often does, in accepting both as true. This does not mean a little of each, but both, entirely. On the one hand, God and only God is responsible for everything that exists in the world, but on the other hand, so are we, and only we! Our minds cannot wrap themselves around this contradiction.

In fact, though, there is no contradiction. One is the "garment" of the other. The power, wisdom, and initiative which we attribute to ourselves are entirely ours, but they are also entirely God's.

The text says *My power and the might of my hand'*. "My power" exists, as does "the might of my hand". We have muscles and strength with which we build, move, create and do. But this strength is not our own. It does not belong to us. It does not belong, period.

The sin is the illusion of ownership. More precisely, it is in the misidentification of the source. Even more precisely, it is in misidentification of the "me" who is the source of strength.

What defines "me"? Is it my skin, my molecular makeup, my organs, the parts of my body? What if I lose one – will I still be me? Am I my talents, my skills, my soul, my actions, my family, my people? Am I the sum of all of these?

The essence of the sin is in shallow and partial identification of "me." Who is speaking in first person in the verse *My power and the might of my hand'*?

I would like to suggest three possibilities:

The first, which I have already alluded to, is that there is not really any "me" at all, because everything has a motivating source ad infinitum.

The second is that there is one true, all-encompassing "Me", as in "I am the Lord your God".

The third is that determinism, as discussed previously, is an entirely false notion and it is the sin itself. Most of us use determinism as the linear basis for our thoughts and actions, as does most of the Western world. Science needs it to prove its theories.

But what if (sit down and take a deep breath), what if each phenomenon is the reason for itself? What if everything is both the source and the essence of itself? Everything is an entire universe unto itself; every phenomenon is both the manifestation of itself and the entire world – everything is actually a manifestation of God!

Following this way of thinking, there is no *'My power and the might of my hand'*, there is only the thing itself – the house, the possession, the money, the herd of sheep – which is a result of itself! Every one of these things is God's creation in the present, every moment anew.

This idea is hinted at throughout the parasha: *"Your raiment waxed not old upon you, neither did your foot swell, these forty years."* How can this be??? It isn't logical, deterministic or even possible! You may say "this is just a biblical tale." I don't think so.

I think this is the essence of the entire Torah – it is in the present, and therefore is not subject to linear, deterministic time.

Parashat Re'eh:
Selective Hearing, Selective Blessing

Parashat Re'eh begins with these words:

"Behold [literally: see/observe]*, I set before you this day a blessing and a curse: the blessing, if you shall hearken unto the commandments of the LORD your God, which I command you this day; and the curse, if you shall not hearken unto the commandments of the LORD your God, but turn aside out of the way which I command you this day, to go after other gods, which you have not known."* (Deuteronomy 11:26-28)

Just two weeks ago, in Parashat Va'etchanan, we received one sensory commandment – Hear (Oh Israel), and now we receive a second: Behold (See). It is far easier to close one's eyes and not see than to close one's ears and not hear. And yet we commonly fault each other on our selective hearing. Perhaps because it is so difficult to filter out sound, that there is a mechanism that allows us to choose what we want to hear, compensating for not being able to block out sounds.

Vision is considered much more reliable (or at least was, in the pre-Photoshop days). Eyewitnesses are usually regarded as more credible than those who simply heard. As children we played "broken telephone", which helped prove that we can't trust our hearing. Rumors are based on untrustworthy hearing, hence gossip is frowned upon.

In this parasha both sight and sound are used: It begins with "Behold" (see), and continues with: "the blessing if you shall hearken…(and) the curse if you shall not hearken." It seems that selective hearing is the source of divine blessing!

None of us know with absolute and objective certainty what God commanded on Mount Sinai. At that dramatic event each person heard the Divine differently, each according to their ability and spiritual stature; each according to his or her personality and soul. Since then and throughout the ages, Jews have debated among themselves what it was that God said. I would like to suggest a radical idea: that God did not say SOMETHING, rather He said absolutely EVERYTHING. Even Moshe heard more than one version of the Ten Commandments – they appear differently in Va'etchanan, which we read two weeks ago, and Yitro, which we read in the winter. On Erev Shabbat we open the Lecha Dodi hymn (written by Rabbi Shlomo Halevi Alkabetz, a Safed Kabbalist, in the 16th century in Tzfat) with the line: "Observe and recall in a single utterance, the One God had uttered unto us", because in one version of the fourth commandment the Torah tells us "Observe the Sabbath" and in the other "recall (or remember) the Sabbath". Only God could say both at once – we humans have selective hearing, hence we must divide the utterance into two different words that we can comprehend.

God said EVERYTHING that was or will ever be said, but we could not and cannot hear it all. Therefore, it is astounding that we are being commanded to HEAR. It must be assumed, therefore, that it is because our hearing is limited by our humanity, we should follow what **we** - selectively - are able to hear.

What a thought! Rabbis who decide on Halacha always consider the important principle - that the laws must be within the limits of human ability to follow, otherwise people cannot hear them. They are simply beyond their pitch. They cannot be comprehended, cannot be heard and cannot be followed.

How does this principle apply to sight? Is our sight objective, as opposed to our subjective hearing? Well, yes and no. Our eyes only take in information, and in that sense our eyes are objective. Yet, it is our brain that processes it, and therefore when we share what we see, we really share a well-processed and digested interpretation of what our physical eyes saw so objectively.

What is this interpretation based on? Our parasha suggests that our vision is based on our hearing:

HEAR, and follow what you hear so that you may SEE blessings! In other words, if you are true to what you HEAR and faithfully follow the Voice YOU heard from on high - as opposed to lowly gossip and chatter, for instance - then you will SEE blessings.

Most of us have absorbed in a very limited and selective fashion the teachings of what is right and what is wrong from our elders. Why are we surprised, then, when blessings are not forthcoming?

Rabbi Nachman reminds us time and again, that the gap between curse and blessing in our lives parallels the gap between our commitment to uphold that which we HEARD and ALREADY KNOW, on the one hand, and our tendency to deny it on the other. He says that all we need to know we already HEARD at Sinai - each and every one of us. We only need to recall it and commit to that SUBJECTIVE AND PERSONAL truth we heard. (Only those who are able to do so may rise to the next level of commitment that awaits them: that of listening to the One OBJECTIVE AND NON-PERSONAL truth, but we will leave that for another time. None of us have reached that level yet.)

Blessings and curses are like a faithful mirror that does not deceive. It reflects accurately not what we want to SEE, but what we want to HEAR! We so badly want to hear that we are good and worthy, but the mirror sometimes reflects a different reality. It reflects back to us the painful gap between what we were ABLE TO HEAR and that which we are willing to carry out.

We are at a special time in the Jewish annual cycle: the seven weeks between consolation (the Shabbat after Tisha B'Av), and personal accounting (Rosh Hashana). Our task is not to learn anything new; just to check whether we are faithful to what we already personally and subjectively HEARD at Mount Sinai, to what we already KNOW. Or not.

Parashat Shoftim: The Gates of Mercy

The marvelous Parashat Shoftim is our focus this Shabbat. The division of civil authority comes from here –a king, a judge, a law enforcer, and even a high court supervising the entire system:

*"You shall appoint magistrates and law enforcers for your tribes, **in all of your gates** that the Lord your God is giving you, and they shall govern the people with due justice. You shall not judge unfairly: you shall show no partiality; you shall not take bribes, for bribes blind the eyes of the discerning and upset the plea of the just. Justice, justice shall you pursue, that you may thrive and live and inherit the land which the Lord your God is giving you."* (Deuteronomy 16:18-20)

The form of the verbs in Hebrew has undergone a transformation from the previous parashot. Deuteronomy begins with Moshe speaking in the plural: "The Lord our God spoke to **us** at Horev..." Now Moshe is speaking in the singular - although the English does not reflect the change. This is a source of confusion in the Hebrew as well: Is Moshe saying that *every*one should appoint magistrates and law enforcers? How could such a thing work, unless his intention was that each person appoints a metaphorical authority over his domain, in which he is able to conduct him or herself with justice and morality? Many interpreters suggest that the instruction is for public figures within a general judicial system, but remind us that we are each personally responsible to honor and respect them.

Another question arises: why "in **all** of your gates"? Why not just "your gates"? Rashi suggests that the intent here is to clarify that all kinds of settlements are included in this guideline, including the

Levite cities of refuge. Everywhere people live together there will be a need for magistrates and law enforcement.

As usual, I prefer to look at Hassidic interpretations, which seek inner applications of these instructions, based on the idea that a person is a microcosm of the universe. This point of view does not contradict others, but enhances them, saying that what happens internally and externally are irrevocably linked, and in order to improve one's surroundings one must begin inside. This explains the use of the singular form of the verbs. Moshe is appealing to each and every person, calling on him or her to place "magistrates and law enforcers" at their gates.

Why at one's gates? What is a gate? Wouldn't one's heart be a more accurate location?

Our inner world is full of incredibly powerful forces. Deep within us there is probably a Divine order, but what we usually sense is chaos and upheaval; conflicting forces which feel much more real and frightening than a seemingly- unattainable inner peace. Are we being asked to tame these forces? I don't think so. I believe they are the force of life in all of its untidy glory, and that is as it should be. Taming it would amount to repression, which is not the goal at all. What we are being asked to do is to guard and tame our "gates". This, too, is very, very hard, but a very reasonable request. I am being asked to take responsibility for what goes in and what comes out of me:

I am responsible for what I choose to see and to hear.
I am responsible for the gossip I hear or repeat.
I am responsible for the way in which I express my anger.
I am responsible for the way in which I express my urges.

Gates are gathering places, both historical and sociological. In biblical times the elders, the wise men and judges used to sit at the city gates, there problems were brought to them to settle: monetary and marital disputes, weddings and divorces, etc. Therefore, the gates were, in fact, the place where human relations were acted out.

On a personal level, our physical gates are the means with which we meet others – our eyes, our mouths, nose, hands, feet, pores. These are the gates where what is internal meets the external. There is much power contained in these meetings!

Last week we marked the first day of Elul, the month of self-reckoning and seeking forgiveness. Parashat Shoftim gives us the means with which to take stock both of the past, and especially to plan for the future of our "gates":

What and how do I want to see?
What and how do I express myself?
What should I eat and drink, and how much?
What am I willing to hear? To smell?
What and how should I touch and feel?

Controlling our gates is hard work, but it is possible!
The initials of the word Elul are often interpreted as "Ani Ledodi Vedodi Li"– Elul is the time of year when "I am my beloved's and he (or she) is mine." Lovers, be they either human or Divine, meet at the gates (as in the hymn Eshet Chayil and in Song of Songs), as do all of God's creatures.

Our goal in the next month or so is to get to the point at which our own gates are so well in hand, that the Divine Gates of Mercy will open up wide and receive us. Expecting them to do so and expecting any positive change to happen without doing our own inner work

202

seems futile and even infantile. If we focus on our own individual gates, both the external and the Higher Gates will reflect our inner work.

Let's do it!

Parashat Ki Tetzeh: The Sanctity of Diversity

Parashat Ki Tetzeh, the sixth parasha in Deuteronomy, contains many commandments which deal with a wide range of topics. It is difficult to find a common thread among them, except that the commandments in the parasha all deal with mitzvot between people; they deal with us, the common people. Some of the mitzvot seem logical to modern sensibilities and even inspirational, while others are not clear to us at all.

One of the less-logical and less observed mitzvot is "Kil'ayim" – mixing - between species of plants, textiles, kinds of animals, grafting fruit trees together, and more. This theme was covered in depth in Vayikra (Leviticus) and reappears here, signifying that it is a matter of great significance.

"A woman must not put on man's apparel, nor shall a man wear woman's clothing... You shall not sow your vineyard with a second kind of seed... You shall not plow with an ox and an ass together. You shall not wear cloth combining wool and linen." (Deuteronomy 22: 5-11)

In an era of genetic engineering, agricultural hybridization and continuous attempts to improve species and crops, the Kil'ayim prohibition is difficult to understand or accept. Added to these are the acceptance of LGBT unions, making the prohibition of mixing and blurring of identities a topic worthy of further investigation and most importantly, requiring interpretation for our times.

Most traditional commentators such as Rashi and Ramban (Nachmanides) claim that the main reason for this prohibition is to keep humans from interfering grossly with the Divine plan, which was declared "good" and even "very good" when first created. However, this "good"-ness is not necessarily used the way we use the term today. It is a concept beyond human understanding of good and bad. Human beings are incapable of seeing the entire picture. Therefore, human interference in one dimension may hinder other dimensions more than help them. It is permissible to improve, suggest traditional commentators, but not to entirely blur the distinctions between what was Divinely created and entirely new creations.

Whether we agree with this logic or not, we can still accept it as a call to pay attention. Beware, because in addition to the wonders of technology (without which this drasha could not be sent to you), we also see, feel and smell the destructive results of man's interference with nature.

This year I would like to focus on one of the "mixtures", "Kil'ayim" that is mentioned in our parasha, a mixture that sounds completely logical and even inspiring: *"Do not plow with an ox and a donkey together."*

This commandment is set in a period when beasts of burden were hitched to plows, in order to drag them through the field. The plow was heavy by necessity, because it needed to have the weight to make furrows in the hard soil. Oxen were most suited for this work, whereas donkeys were more prevalent and cheaper to purchase and to maintain. Donkeys, however, can only bear lighter loads, and do not work well together – an interesting fact I learned this week – whereas oxen and horses do. A rich farmer would have no problem hitching two of his oxen together to work, but a poor farmer may be tempted to hitch his one ox to a donkey.

Although it may seem that the donkey will add a bit of power to the job, this is a misconception which is the basis for understanding the whole concept of "Kil'ayim".

Combining these forces - ox-power and donkey-power - is like operating an electric appliance using different size batteries. The work of an ox is not the work of a donkey. If it was, the expensive ox would not be necessary.

On a humane level, this combination would be a terrible abuse of the animals. The expectation that a donkey can work at the same pace and with the same burden as an ox is cruel, and will cause the donkey much hardship. The donkey is also being forced to work as a team, which is against his nature. Furthermore, it places an extreme burden on the ox, which is made to carry the entire load, and possibly even carry the weight of the donkey.

This, then, becomes a discussion about expectations and about accepting reality as it was created. Any attempt to force an unnatural burden may cause destruction, or at least great pain.

Humans by nature want more, continuously. More and more. Human beings never have enough. The basic human condition is one of a sense of lack, which can exist regardless of actual shortage of anything in particular. The feeling of satiety is fleeting. If one has "everything", he will be worried about losing it, and therefore return to the cycle of sensing deficiency. That's just the way it is; it is the way humanity developed. From the dawn of history, hunger and the sense of deficiency have driven the wheels of creation.

Our creativity, too, has its limits. In Jewish tradition these limits are called "din" – laws of what is permissible and what is prohibited. Din is understood today as judgment. In our case, however, the limits set by the prohibition of mixing do not have the quality of judgment at all, but rather of chessed, kindness. These limits help us identify what we are and are not able to do within the confines of society; hence they are a gift of great compassion. The laws of "Kil'ayim" offer an acknowledgement of reality without judgment. A donkey is a donkey, and an ox is an ox. Each is complete in itself, with its own abilities. Don't impose expectation of the one on the other.

Rationally, we all know that each person is a unique individual, but emotionally we constantly compare ourselves to others based on any number of parameters: income, looks, education, manners – the list is endless. It begins at the well-baby clinic, where we bring our children for postnatal checkups. The checkup is really a series of comparisons. While based on essential health data, they also fulfill a destructive role in subverting the self-esteem of parent and child. This is further strengthened by each test at school, and each grade given. Our worth and that of others is measured against expectations, never against the thing itself, because then it would lack the element of being a test, and tests are always about comparisons.

Try to notice how many comparisons you make in one hour. Every look, every piece of information is processed in our feverish minds, and almost always the process goes like this: "Hmmm, what does this remind me of? Is it more like… or like….? Why isn't it like …? It's nicer, but not really… It needs more … so that it can be more …."

I am not suggesting that we should avoid comparisons. We need markers to measure our wellbeing. However, we are in the month of Elul, the month of forgiveness and reckoning. This can be a good time (only if you wish!) to examine the comparisons we make and the suffering and anxiety they cause us. Miraculously, letting go of these comparisons makes way for great forgiveness!

The laws of Kil'ayim guide us in respecting Creation as it is, without judgment. The Divine court already determined: it is already "good", even "very good"! The laws of Kil'ayim provide us with great clarity, enabling us to see that everything is first and foremost simply itself; not more, not less. It is possible to experience wonder without making comparisons!

True, it is difficult, because we are deeply enmeshed in a system of criticism and judgment, replete with habits of comparison which we learned from the baby clinics onwards, throughout our lives. But this is the purpose of the Torah, and the purpose of the month of Elul.

Since I mentioned the LGBT communities earlier in this drasha, I will return to that topic and say that in the spirit of this interpretation of the parasha, every being is whole and perfect as it is, leaving no need for judgment, just a deep acceptance of the variety and the magic of Divine Creation. Variety is perhaps one of the great secrets of Creation - variety in nature and among people – because it is the ultimate expression of the endless faces of the Creator. Just as we are commanded to observe Kil'aim, we are also commanded to preserve species - human, animal, and plants - and to avoid extinction of diversity.

Parashat Ki Tavo:
Everywhere I Go, I Go to Eretz Yisrael

Ki Tavo is a very beautiful parasha! It has many difficult parts for those of us who do not like to be scolded or warned, but nevertheless it is a parasha that can just about stand alone as a Torah for one's life.

Even the authors of the Hagaddah saw in this parasha an important "mantra" for our collective memory, and chose to quote it in the main part of the Hagaddah, the Maggid (highlighted here in bold letters):

"And it shall be, when (if) *you **come** in unto the land which the LORD your God gives you for an inheritance, and you possess it, and dwell therein; that you shall **take** of the first of all the fruit of the ground, which you shall **bring** in from your land that the LORD your God gives you; and you shall put it in a basket and go unto the place which the LORD your God shall choose to cause His name to dwell there. And you shall **come** unto the priest that shall be in those days, and say unto him: 'I profess this day unto the LORD your God, that I am **come** unto the land which the LORD swore unto our fathers to give us.' And the priest shall take the basket out of your hand, and set it down before the altar of the LORD your God. And you shall speak and say before the LORD your God: **'A wandering Aramean was my father, and he went down into Egypt, and sojourned there, few in number; and he became there a nation, great, mighty, and populous. And the Egyptians dealt ill with us, and afflicted us, and laid upon us hard bondage. And we cried unto the LORD, the God of our fathers, and the LORD heard our voice, and saw our affliction, and our toil, and our oppression. And the LORD brought us forth out of Egypt with a mighty hand,***

and with an outstretched arm, and with great terribleness, and with
*signs, and with wonders. And He has **brought** us into this place,*
*and has **given** us this land, a land flowing with milk and*
honey. *And now, behold, I **have brought** the first of the fruit of the*
land, which You, O LORD, has given me.' And you shall set it down
before the LORD your God, and worship before the LORD your
God." (Deuteronomy 26: 1-10)

The parasha opens with the ambiguous condition: "If" or "when" you
come into the Land..." The implication is – it may not happen!

There is another hint in the same sentence, that the mission is not yet
complete: "come into the Land"; why not "arrive in the Land"?
Arriving implies the end of a journey, whereas coming indicates a
direction, but it does not have the finality of reaching a destination,
as with a GPS. This journey may even be eternal, but it has a
direction which is also eternal.

The opening sentences of the parasha quoted above also contain
many words associated with movement. I have marked them, too, in
bold letters. Although the many verbs emphasize movement, they
do not express arrival: "come," "take," "brought down," "bring,"
"brought"... Perhaps these are all meant as a warning: don't think
that you are arriving somewhere. You are fortunate in that you are
not – you are on a journey.

Why is coming to the Land conditional? Maybe because most of us
are concerned with arriving and not with coming. The Torah is
inviting us to distinguish between an awareness of direction and
movement, and an awareness of arrival.

One of Rabbi Nachman's famous quotes is "Everywhere I go, I go to
Eretz Yisrael." The human journey has been discussed repeatedly in

these drashot. Eretz Yisrael is a metaphor for a destination; not a physical destination necessarily, but rather a compass point. In the pagan world all roads led to Rome. In the Jewish world they lead to Eretz Yisrael. But whereas Rome is a specific, physical place, Eretz Yisrael symbolizes the act of being on a journey.

Rabbi Nachman's famous visit to Eretz Yisrael in 1798 changed his point of view entirely. So much so that he asked that everything he had written prior to the visit be burned. On the other hand, Rabbi Nachman never bothered to get to Jerusalem! After visiting Haifa and Tiberias, he returned to the boat in Akko and with it to Europe!

It was as if he realized that he did not want to arrive. He wanted to come. His statement clarifies that not only do we never arrive; we are in a permanent state of coming.

Most of us frequently feel that we are not on the right path. We seem to be either at a dead end, or heading in a direction that was somehow forced upon us. Rabbi Nachman suggests that this is not possible. One is always on one's path. True, sometimes it is difficult and frustrating, but that does not mean you have left your path. You actually can't! Whatever path you are on *is* yours!

Let's take a closer look at the wonderful statement that the bearer of produce says to the Cohen when bringing his first fruits: *"A wandering Aramean was my father, and he went down into Egypt"*. This is very unclear. Who is the father? Avraham? But he never ended up settling in Egypt. Perhaps then it was Yaakov? But he wasn't an Aramean (he was a Sabra!) Lavan was the Aramean. Why the confusion?

Because our collective story, which is also our own personal story, begins with a journey. Both Avraham and Yaakov go to Egypt and

211

both become very rich and successful. However, Yaakov and his descendants are so successful that they abandon Avraham's journey, **thus they become enslaved by the notion of having arrived**. From the depths of their anguish they cry out for help, and it comes in the form of **movement**, as described in our parasha. The God of movement sends them back to the journey mode.

Therefore, (we say) dear Cohen, I come to you today to bring you the first fruits of my land. I know where it has come from, and I know what my story is. I know that, just like everyone else, I sometimes get lost, as do all human beings. But I continue to search for the way. Many times I have enslaved myself, but with the help of that power that brought my forefathers out of the land in which they were mired, I, too, was released. And here, I have come and I always will, but I will never arrive. I know this land is not mine. I remember it again on this day, and remember, too, that the moment I mistakenly think it (or any other land) is mine I am once again enslaving myself and losing my direction.

So, dear Cohen, I have come to give gratitude for the abundance.

"This day the LORD your God commands you to do these statutes and ordinances; you shall therefore observe and do them with all your heart, and with all your soul. You have affirmed the LORD this day to be your God, and that you would walk in His ways, and keep His statutes, and His commandments, and His ordinances, and hearken unto His voice." (26:16-17)

God's name in Hebrew - Y.H.V.H. - is made up entirely of vowels that flow and move. I am always struck by the commandment to "walk in His ways."
Not stand.
Not arrive.

Just to come.
To walk.
To go down.
To come out.

The Hebraic/Jewish formula for Life is to know how to give thanks, to release, to know that it isn't ours, to continue. *"And you shall rejoice in all the good which the LORD your God has given to you, and to your house, you, and the Levite, and the stranger that is in the midst of you."*

We are asked to do this very difficult task daily. We can do it, our parasha this week tells us, because we are an "Am Segula". Am Segula means neither better, nor smarter; not even more moral. It means "Mesugal" - capable. Capable of reminding itself that there is no final destination, just an ongoing journey - sometimes a wandering - to Eretz Yisrael. The secret to eternal journeying in our parasha is gratitude, gratitude to the One upon whose Land we wander. Are we capable of that too?

Parashat Nitzavim-Vayelech: The Secret of Renewal

Outside it is still hot, but autumn is in the air, and Parashat Nitzavim echoes within us as we near the end of the yearly cycle. Parashat Nitzavim is among the most beautiful – as are all of the parashot, because each in its turn is the ultimate parasha.

Tradition has it that Nitzavim takes place on the last day of Moshe's life. Before the sun sets he will ascend Mount Nevo, look at the endless expanses of the Promised Land and receive a kiss of death. But there is no hint in the parasha that Moshe is preoccupied with his imminent death. We don't know what he is thinking about death. Is he scared?

In my imagination Moshe knows that the end of the current journey is just the beginning of another one, and this enables him to accept his death. In my imagination, a person who knows how to truly surrender and be accepting is able to die as Moshe does, with a kiss of death. This is how Moshe is able to speak about the eternity of the Jewish people, even though he himself will not be around to savor it. The clearest hint that Moshe knows that life as we know it is just the tip of the iceberg appears in this parasha:

"I make this covenant with its sanctions not with you alone, but both with those who are standing here with us this day before the Lord our God, and with those who are not with us here this day." (Deuteronomy 29:13-14)

Who are those "who are not with us here this day", and are still partners to the covenant? Most interpreters agree that the reference is to the generations to come. In other words, the renewed covenant in Deuteronomy is not just with Bnei Yisrael who are about to enter the

Land, but with everyone who will be born to this People in the future. I would like to suggest that the reference here is not to an event that is part of the past or the future. The covenant described here is timeless. It belongs to eternity. The words "this day" are eternal.

How so, you may wonder. Isn't "this day" a very specific, defined time? Today is not in the past or in the future; it is in the present, although it also describes time. The fact is that we can read this sentence every year, and yet "this day" remains the same – it is always there.

Notice how many times the words "this day" appear in the following verses:

*"You stand **this day** all of you before the Lord your God…to enter into the covenant of the Lord your God, which the Lord your God is concluding with you **this day**…that He may establish you **this day** as His people and be your God…"I make this covenant with its sanctions not with you alone, but both with those who are standing here with us **this day** before the Lord our God and with those who are not with us here **this day**.*" (Deuteronomy 29:9-14)

Most of us are not truly engaged in this covenant, because most of us are not "standing here this day". We are slaves of the past and the future, whereas the covenant of "this day" is one of freedom.

The Exodus from Egypt is also an exodus from the dimension of time so revered by the Egyptians that they worshiped Ra, the sun god, and embalmed their bodies for all (human) time. By leaving Egypt, we enter the dimension of the eternal, as we are reminded in the following verses:

"Well you know that we dwelt in the land of Egypt and that we passed through the midst of various other nations; and you have seen the detestable things and the fetishes of wood and stone, silver and god, that they keep. Perchance there is among you some man or woman, or some clan or tribe, whose heart is even now turning away from the Lord our God to go and worship the gods of those nations..." (15-17)

The name of this parasha is the key to experiencing freedom: Nitzavim, standing and being present, declaring "I am here!"

There is a corresponding term for Nitzavim in the Divine dimension, and it too appears in the quote above, in verse 13: Anochi, meaning "I am". The Ten Commandments begin with "Anochi, I am the Lord your God", followed by the next nine commandments. There is a Hassidic tale which relates that what Moshe really heard were not the entire Ten Commandments but only the word, "Anochi", within which all of the commandments and perhaps all of the Torah potentially lay.

I would like to suggest that the words "I am" may be the key to our capacity for renewal, and that this is the reason this parasha always comes before Rosh Hashana.
"Anochi" has an additional meaning in Hebrew. It means "vertical". So, while time is linear and depicted as horizontal (as in timelines), "I am", Anochi, is vertical. It takes place continuously – now, today, at this moment. It is created again and again in each moment, without past or future. This is why the God of Israel is not limited by the dimension of time, which He created.

The freedom of "I am" is available to all, regardless of religion, color, gender, or preference. King Solomon wrote in Kohelet how futile it is to expect the hierarchy of privilege to be permanent.

Everything is fleeting, says Kohelet. Therefore, freedom is to be found in the present, in being here now; in "I am."

How can this be done? It requires a deep shift of consciousness and a lot of practice. The shift is not difficult, but it is entirely foreign to the culture of human thought which is bound by time. This is why we are told to remind ourselves daily to leave Egypt, to stand before our God, the God of the present, who continuously says "I am."

Those of you who are familiar with my drashot are also familiar with my "obsession" with the first question man was asked (and failed to answer): "Ayeka - where are you?" Avraham, the first Hebrew, was the first to answer the question with "Hineni", meaning "I am here." This was the basis of Abraham's covenant with God, and it echoed God's words, "I am." But then our forefathers went down to Egypt and the covenant was forgotten. Moshe renewed it at Sinai, and again, 40 years later, in this week's parasha, together with Am Yisrael.

To stand in front of God, to know how to say "I am here" to God's "I am" is the most worthy way to end the month of Elul. I know no way more precise or pure in which to be renewed.

A Blessing from the Depths for the New Year:

From Avraham of the Bible, to Avraham Maslow,
to Rabbi Avraham Yitzchak HaCohen Kook

I have wondered, as the New Year approaches, what blessing to bestow on my loved ones, my congregation and all of those whom I have contact with. And if I am already at it, perhaps I can even seek a blessing for myself.

But what is this blessing that we bless each other on the High Holidays? Do we have the power to impact reality, maybe even to change the future? Do blessings have power? If not, what is their purpose? Maybe good wishes such as "Have a good day" are not much more than social pleasantries and not really blessings, and now we simply extend them from one day to an entire year, and say: "Have a sweet New Year."

So, will the coming year be, in fact, sweeter because we said so?

I would like to suggest that people exchange blessings (as opposed to blessings bestowed by God) as an act of fine-tuning and declaring intention.

From Rav Kook's writings I have learned that blessings are hidden within the process of clarifying one's deepest desires. This is because our desires fuel the mechanism through which life energy flows. The premise of Jewish tradition is that at the root of every one of our desires is the wish to match them with that of the Creator. In Sayings of the Fathers (2:4) it says – *"Make His will your own, so that your will and His will become one. Submit your will to His, so that He will match the will of others to meets yours."*

Therefore, the first blessing I wish to bless us with is that of a renewed acquaintance with our deepest desires. In other words, that we should know what we really want. A person who knows what he wants, whether because he is naturally in tune with him or herself or because he was raised in a family that enabled him to differentiate between fleeting wishes and deep, authentic desires, or whether as a result of a conscious effort to discover his unique will – such a person is closer to the source of blessing because he is attuned to the Divine Will.

What will we discover as the essence of our will? Is it the same for all people?

Avraham Maslow determined self-actualization to be the highest-ranking psychological need in his famous pyramid of needs.

Various spiritual and religious traditions identify a different need or desire as the most significant: that of Oneness. According to these traditions, the hidden hand steering human life is that of longing for connection, for oneness. The Greeks called this longing "Eros", and in Latin it is called "Intimacy", located – according to Edgar Levenson the theoretician - "most within".

Jewish tradition has given this longing many names, such as "holiness" (meaning intimacy with what is Divine and what is human) and "One(ness)", (as in "Hear oh Israel, the Lord our God, the Lord is One" and prayers such as "On that day He will be one and His name will be One"). Therefore, I believe that the desire for closeness, for oneness, is at the root of human desire, or in Maslow's terms, at the top of the pyramid of needs.

The longing for closeness, for intimacy – in its deepest and widest sense – motivates human development, be it scientific-technological, spiritual-philosophical, or artistic. With modern technology, the ability to be in contact with friends, family members, community, and even with people elsewhere in the world has never been simpler. So are the technical options for self-actualization for people of all kinds.

And yet it appears that alienation and loneliness are also at an all-time high in the Western world. The classic community structure - the village, the kibbutz, the neighborhood, the shteibel – even the family unit, which was the basis for intimacy, have all unraveled.

I am a big believer in a Higher Plan, a plan that we do not understand. Perhaps the unraveling of traditional social structures is part of it, but as I have no way of knowing; my words here are purely speculation or intuition. The unraveling of traditional structures frees us to find deeper sources of intimacy, sources that used to be considered selfish or egocentric. We may come closer to ourselves, to the God of our hearts, to our bodies, to the innermost places of our existence.

Rav Kook's writings deal extensively with this notion. He calls it "T'shuva", from the word "Lashuv", to return home, to ourselves. He was not scared of using the word "I" and "Me", and didn't see them as a threat to collective good. He was ahead of his time, and it seems his time has come.

The year that has drawn to a close contained a great deal of insanity. It seems humanity is again on the move, and we may be only at the very beginning of a larger, complex process. One thing we can do when the world goes crazy is to draw closer to ourselves, to our sources of strength, to the anchor that is always at our disposal in times of uncertainty.

Therefore, I would like to take this traditional opportunity, on the occasion of the New Year, to bless us all with the ability to come closer to ourselves; to attune our inner compass to intimacy with ourselves, which will allow us to come closer to others near or far. May it be a year of complete T'shuva – to ourselves, to our God, to the energizing springs of life which are hidden within all of us.

Yom Kippur: Come in, Come in... and be Blessed!

In Temple times, Yom Kippur was a very dramatic day. It was exciting, impressive and exalting. On that day – and only on that day – the High Priest (and only the High Priest) would enter the Holy of Holies!

There are those who say that the goal of the impressive ceremony was to cause the nation to forgive and be forgiven. Only forgiveness and atonement would guarantee a year of blessing. Yet, although both are very important, I am not sure they are the goal but rather the means towards something else.

What we have here is an ancient rite whose essence is entering the depth of holiness into the beating pulse at the center of the world, and then emerging safely back into the world of action and creativity.

My regular readers may notice that once again, I am writing about a journey inwards. My apologies, but this is the only worthy journey I know of. Every parasha, each holiday, event, law, breath, and step – they are all variations or aspects of human yearning inwards. The Yom Kippur ceremony guarantees us that he, or she, who successfully journeys inwards will emerge safely with a great blessing, the blessing of a good year. The greeting "May you be written and signed for a good year" turns into "Shana Tova" at the end of Yom Kippur.

Everything that concerns us in our lives has many layers. These layers serve to bring us either closer or farther from the heart of the issue, from its essence. Like concentric ripples in the water which are located at various distances from the place at which the stone lands. The innermost circle is closest to the source, while the most distant one is the widest and most remote. Anyone who has undergone a psychological journey is familiar with the power of touching upon deep feelings, the sources of both pain and pleasure. And, on the other end of the spectrum, we are also all too familiar with our tendency to chatter about things when we are actually very distant from their essence.

Here are the main stages of the ancient ceremony. The description is taken from parashat "Acharei Mot" in Leviticus, which we read Yom Kippur morning. The minute details of the ceremony do not, however, appear in the Torah, but rather in the Mishna, in Masechet Yoma, which deals with the laws of Yom Kippur. Seven days prior to Yom Kippur the High Priest (the Cohen Gadol) would leave his home and go to the Temple grounds in order to begin preparations for the big day. The preparations were both professional and spiritual. The blessing for the entire nation was his responsibility. The day before Yom Kippur he had to swear that he would change nothing in the established procedures of the "Avoda" service. The night before, they would make sure he did not fall asleep, lest he dream and have an emission, rendering him impure and unable to perform his holy task the following morning.

In the course of the "Avoda" ceremony he would change his clothes five times, bathing in the mikveh to purify himself in between each one. In the course of the very long day, the Cohen Gadol performs 39 different actions, all in perfect order and detail: He lights the menorah, first with five and then with two more candles; he offers three different kinds of sacrifices – for himself and his family, for all of the Cohanim, and for all of Israel; he sprinkles blood in various places, very precisely; he prepares the incense, lights it, places it, collects it, and so on.

223

One of the climaxes of the ceremony was that of the two goats, a procedure which is very hard for modern sensibilities to comprehend. All of the sins of Israel were ceremoniously placed on the goats by the Cohen Gadol. One of them was then sacrificed on the altar, and the other sent into the desert.

Undoubtedly the most terrifying moments of the day were when the Cohen Gadol entered the Holy of Holies. The assumption was that if he was not pure enough, if he had not been precise enough in his preparations for the ceremony, if his intentions were not completely accurate, he would not survive that very intimate moment. The collective memory of the Cohanim was seared by the harsh fate of the two sons of Aharon, the first High Priest, who brought a "strange fire" before the altar and were killed by God for their action. This is why the portion we read on Yom Kippur begins immediately following their death. There was so much concern about the safety of the Cohen Gadol, that a rope would be tied around his waist to pull him out should the worst happen and he did not make it out alive.

While in the Holy of Holies, or a moment before he emerged, the Cohen Gadol would pray and beg on behalf of the people, but the absolute climax of the ceremony was when he would say God's name out loud. At that moment of ecstasy all of the Cohanim and the people would "fall on their faces" (bow very low) with great emotion. We no longer know what Divine name was uttered, but to this day the custom of bowing remains in almost all synagogues, including ours, during the Mussaf service.

The 39th stage of the ceremony was the Cohen Gadol leaving the Temple and returning to his home and to his family. All of the people accompanied him on his way, celebrating his emergence together, and blessing his safe return.

So what did we have here? A week of precise and challenging preparations to enter, the great day itself, on which the movement inwards towards the Holy of Holies was completed, ending with the jubilant emergence and return home. What is all of this supposed to mean to us today? What does it have to do with us?

The Hebrew word for the curtain in the Holy of Holies is "**kaporet**", which is unique and seldom used. It contains the roots of the words atone and fertility, as well as being a covering. The male foreskin, "orlah," is also associated with this concept, because of the way it acts as a cover. The same word is the root of "arel", which is used to describe Moshe, whose tongue impeded his speech, and the term "arel lev" which is used to describe someone whose heart is covered so that it renders him without feeling, heartless.

This is the state in which most of us live most of our lives: covered with layers of all types, qualities and densities. However, every person recognizes the feeling of longing which lies beneath those layers. That longing is accompanied by a pain of yearning to go inwards, into the pulsating heart of life, and to meet the Divine there. Going inwards, into the depths, into the sanctuary of the Divine presence, to touch the essence with exposed nerve endings – this is not easy at all! It is so challenging that we often "cheat". In other words, we act as if we are going inwards, when really we are just fooling ourselves. A person who is very emotional or dramatic isn't necessarily deeper or closer to the essence of life than an intellectual or a cynic is. Often the emotion and the drama can be as much of a covering as an excess of analysis can be.

Any desire – even the most superficial, every ideology – even the most bizarre, every urge – even the most bestial, contains longing. We may mistakenly attribute a mythic or even minute truth to these desires, ideologies, and urges, convincing ourselves that they are IT.

225

But they aren't. They never are, because the journey inwards is endless. There is no limit to its depths. There may be temporary satiety, but never an end.

Therefore, the goal of the Cohen Gadol's entrance into the Holy of Holies is not forgiveness. The goal is to enter. In other words, to return inwards, "lashuv", which is why we are now in the Ten Days of T'shuva, of return. We desire to return to a full and satisfying life, and forgiveness is a means to this end. In order to enter our lives and fully live them we must forgive our endless layers that we believed were our essence. They were vehicles for inner exile from ourselves, from our life force. Every sense of guilt, every finger pointed, judgment made, hatred felt create distance. There is no entrance to the Holy of Holies without a deep, total acceptance of reality.

The Temple was destroyed because it became only an external shell. While it is true that every shell contains a yearning for what lies beneath or within it, a shell cannot be called a Temple or a Holy of Holies. The dissonance and the dishonesty of such a combination was too dramatic to exist, and therefore it crumbled.

Yom Kippur is the day on which all curtains, partitions, and coverings are removed.
How can this be done? Jewish tradition invites us to abstain for 25 hours from the main actions with which we encase ourselves (food, drink, and other pleasures). Most of us will be very busy being hungry and thirsty, suffering from a headache and calculating how much time is left. While this is understandable, it misses the point of Yom Kippur. Instead, you can try to imagine delving inwards, into the hunger and the thirst, into the headache. Through them or under them, you may find a trap door that leads to the Holy of Holies.

Anyone who manages to go inwards – no matter how much – and come out safely at the end of the day will bring blessing to him or herself and to our surroundings… a blessing of renewal.

Chag Sameach (yes, we can say this on Yom Kippur, because there is nothing happier than going inwards and coming out safely)!

Wishing those who are fasting a useful fast (let us remember not to judge those who aren't, because judgment creates distance), and may we all find one of the many paths inwards.

Parashat Ha'azinu: Honey from the Rock

On the Shabbat between Yom Kippur and Succot, we read a special poem which has the power to bring us home when we are lost. Parashat Ha'azinu is essentially a beautiful poem, and I am always surprised that it was not included in the siddur as Shirat Hayam (the great poem that was sung after crossing the Red Sea) is. While it is a unique, spiritual poem, it is not easy to understand. But the effort is well worth it!

The God of Parashat Ha'azinu is not an infantile God, one who sits on a cloud and orchestrates the world through scoldings and treats.

The God of Ha'azinu is deep, internal, and present. He enables all of life to flow from Him and to return to Him.

One of my favorite lines in Ha'azinu describes that God: *"... fed him honey from the rock, and oil from the flinty stone."* (D'varim 32:13)

Honey from the rock! Is this possible?

The God that Moshe sings about is infinitely present in every cell, every molecule, every atom, proton and subatomic quark there is an infinite Divine presence. It is a knowing that requires a higher mind and a very open heart. Those who know and understand that everything is made from the very same essence without distinctions of any kind, know, too, with absolute certainty, that it is possible to be fed honey from a rock. Any rock. And that it is also possible to drink oil from a flinty stone.

Shirat Ha'azinu demands that we deepen our perception. It insists that in order to get honey from a rock it is necessary to grow up and stop looking superficially at God as a sugar daddy who hands out gifts to those who are loyal and do what he asks of them. The God of Moses demands that we see His infinite presence in all of Creation. Only then can we be nourished by God's existence at every level and layer of our being.

How fitting it is that we read this on the Shabbat between Yom Kippur and Succot. We have fasted; we have cleansed ourselves of layers of unfulfilled promises and the deceptive idols that ran our lives in the past year. On Erev Succot we will leave our illusion of safety and cement, and spend one week away from the idol of real-estate that has seized the entire country for years. Whether you sleep in your Succah or only eat in it occasionally, let it serve as a reminder of the Divine that is present in every green branch, every citrus fruit, every clump of soil; in the millions of stars shining through the branches when the lights go out.

May it be a year of experiencing God's presence as honey from a rock!

Sukkot – A Journey to Remember

Sukkot is one of the richest holidays in our yearly cycle, loaded with symbolism: the gathering of the harvest ("asif"), the 4 species gripped together, a temporary dwelling, a memory of ancestral pilgrimage, a reminder of our never-ending wandering, the Priestly blessing, the Beit Hashoeva prayers for rain and abundance, the aggressive beating of the willow fronds on Hoshana Rabba, reading Kohelet (Ecclesiastes) on Shabbat Chol Hamoed, and more.

So much in just one week, no wonder God commanded an eighth day!

Sukkot may be the ultimate metaphor for the totality of life and the world. We do not really know the world – we only know our own, human, experience of it. Hence Sukkot carries the essence of the human experience of life and of the world, filled as it is with transience, wandering, and the potential journey from the hidden to the revealed.

Transient? Far worse! Try fleeting, futile and meaningless…

Yet, Sukkot offers great solace and hope in the face of what may seem frightening and destabilizing. In fact, if we fully give ourselves over to Sukkot's calling, life's existential anxiety may indeed be transformed into ultimate joy! Then we will get to fulfill the overarching mitzvah of this festival: "[and you shall] Be happy in your festival. [In fact, you shall] be ONLY happy!"

The Halacha instructs us to build a Sukkah whose shade is greater than its light – enough shade to shelter us from most of the bright rays of the sun, yet enough open space to allow the stars to shine through at night, reminding us that the Infinite is mostly hidden from our human perspective. At best we can see tiny shimmering glimpses of His light.

Sukkot is a tribute to THE human journey, the mythical, albeit 100% real, journey from Mitsrayim to Eretz Zavat Chalav Udvash: no preparation, very little planning, and scraping together whatever materials present themselves to provide shelter and face the challenges life has in store for us. A life in which all is transient.

The Sukkot journey spirals. In my imagination the spiral is heading down, into the depth of our being. In my imagination God is found in the depths, at the core of everything ("from the depths I call out to you"). I know that for many others, the spiral seems to be ascending ("a song of ascent"), rising higher and higher and higher, for God dwells in the upper echelons. We humans come in many shapes, forms, and imaginings of the Divine.

Throughout Sukkot, a somewhat-agonizing whisper accompanies our journey. "Hevel Havalim" it says, "hevel havalim". It is the groan of an ancient and wise king. "Hevel havalim amar Kohelet, hakol havel". Futility and fleeting, said Kohelet, all is transient…

As we ascend or descend on the spiraling journey, the four species appear, species of abundance, and of solace. We gather them into our two hands, clench hard, wave them towards the four corners of our being to give thanks and to celebrate the bounty achieved from the sweat of our brow.

But not from the sweat of our brow alone. The harvest depends so much on rain, and rain is beyond our control, and extremely unpredictable here in Israel. Some years it rains, some years it doesn't. And Egypt is always just a short journey away. Very little rain falls in Egypt, but the Nile never fails to provide sustaining water. Alternatively, there is always the option of returning to the birthplace and homeland of our great Forefather, on the abundant shores of the great Euphrates River in Babylonia. No concern of scarcity there. And indeed, so transient and fleeting is life here that many have found themselves walking humbly in the footsteps of prior generations that sought stability and security in Egypt, Babylonia, New York, Berlin, and the Silicon Valley, to name a few. Stability and abundance are always just a plane ride (and a visa) away.

But Sukkot will send its outstretched arms to us wherever we may be. "Return", it says, "Return". "On the Rivers of Babylon, where we sat down, and there we wept, when we remembered Zion". But what was the Zion that we remembered? Why did we stay and cry? We certainly did not long for the temporary, fleeting earthly delights we left behind. "Not a hunger for bread and not a thirst for water", the prophet answers. Sukkot sends a soft, ancient whisper, reminding us, "Not by bread alone will man live."

Then by what? By what, for heaven's sake?

We don't know. But nevertheless, we start packing. Carrying our few possessions (=D'varim) on the path of T'shuva (=return), we set out again on the journey through the vast wilderness. There is a historical promise out there; a promise of milk and of honey keep us moving forward. A well, filled with drinking water along the way, and a generous oasis with grapevines and fig trees awaits all those who embark on the journey home. So fresh is the water, so sweet are the grapes and the figs, so soothing is the shade, that we forget it is just a temporary stop along the way.

Indeed, the sheltering leaves of the fig trees and the grape vines are not eternal either. In the autumn they dry, shrivel and fall to the ground. "From dust you came, to dust you shall return", yes, even the leaves. And the well that quenches our thirst runs dry by mid-September, patiently awaiting the winter rains to replenish its emptiness.

"To everything there is a season". All is futile, all is fleeting, and "there is nothing new under the sun".

When all is transient, futile and fleeting, the longing for stability and solid ground reawakens. A memory of a promised land - promised so long ago – surfaces in conversations. Legends passed down from generation to generation of its abundant goat milk, and honey flowing from its sweet dates are retold.

Suddenly, years of longing erupt into prayer, Hosha'anot. And the Hosha'anot are beaded together into a tribal dance. Fatigued people gather with willow branches in their hands. Sukkot is almost over and no deliverance is in sight. They are tired of waiting! "Enough!" they call out, as they pound the willow branches on chairs and tables, and even on one another. "Let those transient leaves fall. Enough! Let the eternal solid core appear!"

It is now Hoshanna Rabba. Sukkot is almost over. With leafless branches in hand, the Hosha'anot now turn into a desperate plea for rain and for God's sustenance.

But then something amazing happens. It is no longer important if these prayers are answered or not. They don't need to be. The prayers were never really intended to sway the Creator. Rather, they carried within them a deeper yearning than just for solid ground and security.

It is a yearning for the source of all things.
It is a longing for the Rock of Creation.
It is an ache for the Master of all temporary dwellings.

Everything is transient. Everything is fleeting. Everything is temporary, except the Creator of all that which is transient, fleeting and temporary. For He alone is eternal.

Ahhh… Finally we are knocking on heaven's doors.

Sukkot is virtually over. Many make the mistake and leave just then. It's been seven days. Seven long days. A lifetime. Enough, they say. We want to return to the mundane. But God asks us to remain there, with Him, one more day. Miracles of abundance usually take place on the eighth day. Seven is the number of natural wholeness and abundance in Creation. But eight is eternity. Eight is the covenant. The covenant with eternity is what we were seeking all along. And that's miraculous.

For those who genuinely persist, on the eighth day of the journey the longing may finally awaken their hearts and their eyes.

Look, it says. Nothing is really fleeting. Nothing is temporary at all. Nothing is transient.
Look! The Creator is within every molecule, every atom.
Look! Nothing is void of His presence.
In fact, you didn't really journey at all. For wherever you went, wherever you journeyed, wherever you wandered, He was always there.

But were you???

"And (then) you shall rejoice in your festival, [in fact] you shall be ONLY joyful".

And just as we think that we will never be cast out of His blissful Garden again, for there is no other place but God's garden... someone in the synagogue rises, opens the Holy Ark, and one by one, all the Torahs are taken out. People start dancing, drunk with joy and some alcohol. And when the Torahs are returned to ark, one is carefully placed on the reading Bima... and ... the story returns to the Beginning.

In the Beginning all was fleeting, transient, and temporary.

But wait! Before we lose that joyful bliss that we reached, will we remember this year that in the very Beginning God said: "Behold, all is well. All is good. All that I created is very good!"?

If we can remember that, then this will surely be a delightful year.

Shabbat Chol Hamo'ed Succot:
Kohelet Was a Housewife in Jerusalem

"Futility futility, said Kohelet; futility futility, all is futile." These famous words are read on Shabbat, Chol Hamo'ed Succot in most synagogues. Although Kohelet appears in the Writings, not in the Torah, Our Sages still determined that it be read on this particular Shabbat. It is so appropriate for the temporary and fragile nature of a succah, the feeling of autumn, the moments before the end of the High Holidays and the beginning of a return to routine.

Kohelet, (also known as Ecclesiastes) whom tradition identifies as King Solomon, comes to the conclusion in his old age, that everything he believed in and was confident about is futile or vaporous (which is the literal meaning of ("Hevel"). What wonderful liberation! What human greatness! Yet the price is tremendous: confusion, a loss of direction, a questioning of all the anchors which kept him from being swept away by the storms of life. These are not the words of a young Solomon, the great lover of God and of a thousand wives, the one who wrote the Song of Songs to express this love. Nor are they the words of the mature Solomon, the wisest among men, who wrote his solid insights in Proverbs. The Solomon of Kohelet is an old king who has seen it all, and who dares question freely everything he has seen and thought.

My grandmother of blessed memory was a little bit like Kohelet. She, too, was a queen in Jerusalem. She was not born there and did not take part in any famous battles, yet for about 50 years she was a queen in her modest home. As a cosmopolitan Jewish girl in Prague who dabbled in the Zionist fantasy in her Zionist youth movement, she did not imagine that she would one day really raise a family in the primitive Levant. Even after that reality indeed transpired, with the birth of her first-born child (my mom) she still considered it an unfortunate mistake, soon to be remedied by her speedy return to her beloved Prague. The idea of Eretz Yisrael was a wonderful and romantic one for a youth movement, but there was no reason to get carried away. Idealism had its place, but so did realism. The rise of Hitler changed everything, and brought about her immigration to Israel at the last possible moment. Her parents, who stayed behind did not survive the Holocaust. They could not have imagined that their only daughter, an enlightened and liberated soul, would return wholeheartedly to her Jewish roots, and even become a right-wing supporter of Gush Emunim.

The bitter and loud ideological arguments in her modest Jerusalem kitchen are still clear in my mind and raging in my ears. It was the 70s and then the 80s, when the country was clearly divided between Right and Left; between supporters of Greater Israel and those who believed in exchanging land for peace. We all fought valiantly, but that fragile old woman always had the upper hand. My family and I would come to Jerusalem from our Labor-oriented kibbutz in the northern Galilee (when it was our turn to enjoy the communal kibbutz car for Shabbat). Driving along the Jordan Valley, we promised ourselves that this time we not be trapped into political discussion with Savta, but we always were, despite our better judgment. It took a small, unquenchable comment from any of us, and the ideological fireworks would flare.

My parents and siblings would then go out to visit old friends, and I got to stay with her. She and I had much more important issues to argue about; Oh yes, we had truly holy issues. Our best arguments were about God. I swore there wasn't one, and she insisted there was. I said she was afraid of discovering the truth, that there is nothing beyond, and she – part prophet, part "witch" – warned me that one day I would discover the truth. I was young and

237

enthusiastic, a little like the young Solomon, and she was mature and wise, like the Solomon of Proverbs. By Motse'ei Shabbat the ideological fires were extinguished, as we kissed and hugged, and loaded the car with goodies that my grandmother had prepared for us. Then we would rush back home, to the kibbutz, because the car was needed by someone else the next day.

As the years went by, the closeness between us did not abate, but it did change. I grew up and my grandmother aged. I would visit her and my grandfather frequently in their last years. At that point I was already wearing a kippah on my head, God in my heart, and sparks of belief in my eyes. I was brimming with religious insights, laws, and words of Torah which I was learning in rabbinical school.

Without noticing, I had entered the Proverbs stage of my life, but my grandmother had moved on to the Kohelet stage of hers. I am not exactly sure when it happened, but she would look at me with pleasure – never saying "I told you so!" – while she listened intently to my words of wise enthusiasm. She would the respond with, "yes, maybe"… and "who knows"… I had thought she would be thrilled to hear my latest rabbinic insights, but Kohelet took over and was now in charge. She continued to believe, to pray, and to support Gush Emunim, but her God was no longer the God of Proverbs, and even her belief in the Greater Land of Israel was no longer as fierce. Hers was the God of Kohelet, the God of futility, of vapor. All is futile. There is nothing new and exciting under the sun…

Jerusalem seems to do that to people – kings and housewives alike. Or maybe it was the old-age home, or perhaps old-age itself.

Biographically, chronologically, I should still be in the Proverbs stage, the stage of wisdom and wit, but something in me is not entirely there anymore. Something tells me that everything is, in fact, vaporous. Something whispers in my ear that there is no right and wrong, correct and incorrect. There isn't just one path or even two. There are many. An infinite number. I find myself suspended between the complete confidence of Proverbs and the complete questioning of Kohelet.

Sometimes the Proverbs person in me asks the Kohelet which is taking root: if that's the case, if all is futile, and there is nothing new under the sun, what is the point of getting up in the morning? What is the purpose? If all rivers flow to the sea and the sea does not get full, why bother? Why expend energy and effort? Why write this drasha? For whom and for what? Who cares and who will remember?

Then the Kohelet in me thinks for a moment, yawns, takes a deep breath and says something a bit scary like: "Don't get up for anyone. You're not doing anyone a favor. It is time to stop trying to please everyone; stop expecting a prize for good behavior. There really is no good reason to make an effort." I have a very hard time hearing this, but then Kohelet continues, "Just be completely loyal to your God." "Why?" I ask him. "Because that is all there is. There is nothing else." And then he quotes the dramatic end of the book of Kohelet: ***"The end of the matter, all having been heard: be in awe of God, and keep His commandments; for this is the human condition."***

Shrewd and obscure… Perhaps it should be forbidden to read this megillah before the age of 50. Perhaps anyone who plans to read Kohelet should first pass a maturity test. The test would include a deep examination of a person's readiness to do without his or her anchors, truths, education, everything he or she ever wrote or lectured enthusiastically about.

The Proverbs person in me tries to make sense of the final lines of Kohelet:

"The end of the matter" – after all of the questions and answers, and after all of the smart books you have ever read…

"All having been heard"- …you have heard it all, there is nothing new, been there, done that, and exhausted all those arguments…

"Be in awe of God" – The word for "awe" in Hebrew connotes both fear and seeing- …stop fearing the deceptions of your eyes. Stop fearing altogether. There is nothing and no one to fear, because God is all there is. So instead of being fearful, be in awe. See truly and in wonder. See God everywhere, in everything, because there is nothing else.

"Keep His commandments" – I will not determine here what those commandments are and what constitutes deceptive idol worship. Every person needs to determine this for him or herself. Our Sages gave us a suggestion as to how best to do this. Their advice was to find a wise person, teacher, guide or rabbi, who can help us figure it out, because it is hard to do so on our own.

"For this is the human condition"- …because at the end of the day, that is all there is. The rest is futile. All of our dramas, our loves, our disappointments, all of the stories we ever told ourselves and others, the wars we have fought, the places we have visited, our achievements and medals… it was all good, but it is also all futile. Awe of God is all that's left. All there ever was. And it is a lot. It is everything. It is infinity.

My grandmother, who was once queen of her home in Jerusalem, is now sitting with her parents on the sea to which all rivers flow. They are discussing life, in German, of course – her father is talking about Hitler's rise to power and that the world will surely not let him carry out his crazy ideas, she is telling them about Greater Israel, and about the wonderful family she raised in the Levant, and about Jerusalem. She no longer has to tell them about God. No need to.

240

God is all there is anyway. And they discuss everything calmly, no longer arguing and certainly not shouting, because there is no reason to. Everything has already been heard, and there is no need to be right. All is futile anyway. They can watch from above and see the saddest but most entertaining show in town, eat some delicious strudel, drink some wine and enjoy the total infinity of it all.

L'Chaim Savta!

Zot Habracha & Simchat Torah:
All Who Are Thirsty, Go to the Water

Tonight we leave our Succah and return to our house in the deep, metaphoric sense of the word. Just as we entered the Succah joyously, so, too, we leave it with joy and with dancing.

Tonight the sun will set on the holiday we call "The Season of Our Joy", and seven days of happiness will end. After sunset is the eighth day – Sh'mini Atzeret – and with it an entirely different holiday: Simchat Torah (the joy of the Torah).

What is so joyous about Simchat Torah? There are many reasons to be joyful – some of them religious and belief-based (the belief that God bestowed some of His infinite wisdom on us); some are anthropological-sociological (the Torah is perceived to be the story of our nation regardless of religious affiliation, economic status, gender, or ethnic background). Every person has his or her own relationship with the Torah and a reason to find joy in it. I, too, have a personal reason for joy, and this is what I would like to share with you this year.

I love language. I love the idea that a person creates his world and gives it meaning by such a simple thing as words. Take the combinations of movements of the mouth, tongue, and teeth, add a breath of air and a sound, and there you have it – a word! An entire world has been created, a reality!

It is said of the Torah *"Delve and delve into it, for all is in it;"* (Avot 5:22)

As someone who came to the Torah from "the outside", I was captivated by its magic when I realized that every verse and every word in it contains an infinite number of interpretations and possibilities. Truly an infinite number. For thousands of years the Torah has been studied, interpreted and discussed, and there are always new layers uncovered, layers that were hidden within it. Every generation finds itself reflected in it. Every generation interprets it without difficulty. It has been there in the most authentic, deep way from the time of our Sages who began to interpret it 2400 years ago and distilled a glorious life of the spirit, of morality and actions that have continued from that time and all the way to this very day.

It is because of the infinite number of possible interpretations that the Torah is compared to a spring whose water never ceases to flow. It is a generous spring, ready and willing to satisfy the thirst of anyone willing to plunge into its depths and find meaning in it. It does not distinguish between religious, traditional, and secular, or between man and woman, Jew and non-Jew.

However, this spring is less accessible to those who see it superficially. The simplest reading will produce some chapters which are more interesting and others which are quite boring; chapters which are pleasant to the modern ear and others which will cause us to squirm; paragraphs that are exciting and others that cause us to cringe; verses that are as beautifully composed as a High Court decision, and others that seem like they belong to a primitive nomadic people.

Just as the spring originates deep in the earth, hidden from lazy eyes, so does the life-giving water of the Torah. It makes itself apparent only to those who are willing to delve into it over and over. Those who do will discover that their initial understanding may be reversed, and that the simple (p'shat) reading renders many contradictory, opposing, and exciting possibilities.

In order for the Torah to be a Torah of Life and not just an ethical or legal code, one needs to know how to bring water out of a rock. Striking the rock is a little like peeling off dead skin, but the goal is not discovering what is underneath, but rather the peeling itself. The process is one of interpretation, of renewal, and it never ends. If we do not continue peeling, the old skin dries up and no longer can convey the light within it. I know what it feels like when a person persists in looking in the Torah that which they already know – it's boring, it's draining! There is no life in such learning.

And I know what it feels like when suddenly, from within the text, a new insight emerges; a new connection that is fresh, inspiring, and challenging, as though it has been pronounced by a heavenly voice. In those moments, I can't understand why I haven't seen that particular insight before, since the text itself has remained the same. Then I realize that while the text has remained the same, the reader has not. Today's reader is not the same as yesterday's reader, and the text will always mirror who we are in the present. Even if a heavenly voice had screamed the insight into my ear previously, I would not have heard. A person can only hear that which is in his heart here and now.

Studying Torah – striking the rock, peeling off old layers - this is an art. There are all kinds of artists, and each will draw forth their own unique water from the rock. A person may be born with one talent or another, but he is not born an artist. Artistry requires practice not talent, as does the art of Torah study. (In Hebrew the words for "artist" and for "practice" have the same root.) It requires a determined, preferably gentle, meeting between a person's heart and the heart of the Torah. Then, when the solid rock turns to flesh, the

244

Torah pours forth from the rock in all of its sweetness, freshness, and liveliness.

The prophet Isaiah said: *"Everyone that is thirsty come for water..."* (55:1) Our Sages tried to understand what he was trying to say. Obviously, anyone who is thirsty should go and drink. This discussion gave birth to the following midrash:

Rabbi Hanina Bar Iddi said: Why are the words of the Torah compared to water? To tell us that just as water begins at a high point and flow to a low one, so the words of the Torah are a comfort for those whose thoughts are elevated and flow towards those whose thoughts are low... Just as the water gives life to the world, so the Torah gives life to the world, as it says: "They are life to those who find them..." Just as water revives a person's soul, so, too, do the words of Torah, as it says: The Torah of God is whole and rejuvenates." Just as water flowing from a spring does so at no cost, so the words of Torah "are there for anyone who is thirsty." (Yalkut Shimoni 89).

You are all welcome to join in celebrating the Torah. Come join the dance of our spring of water, and the hakafot of Simchat Torah. If we know how to be joyous on Simchat Torah, we may be worthy of this blessing:

"And he will be like a tree planted on the water side who gives its fruit in its time and its leaves do not wither and all he does succeeds." (Psalms 1:3)

All who are thirsty go to the water!

Made in the USA
Las Vegas, NV
08 May 2021

22674974R00134